THE
COMPLETE
CIGAR
BOOK

THE
COMPLETE
CIGAR
BOOK

ANWER BATI

HarperCollins*Publishers*

First published in Great Britain in 2000 by
HarperCollins
an imprint of HarperCollins Publishers
77-85 Fulham Palace Road
London W6 8JB

www.fireandwater.com

13579108642

ISBN 0-00-710948-2

Editorial director Andrew Duncan
Art director Beverley Stewart
Maps by Chris Foley
Assistant editor Nicola Davies
Proofreader Mark Adcock

FOREWORD

I FIRST VISITED Cuba in 1992. When I returned, I wrote an article for *The Times*, mostly about Havana cigars. At the time I was one of the few British journalists to have written about cigars, and was approached by a publisher as a result of the Times piece. The resulting book, *The Cigar Companion* – first published in 1993 – went to three editions, and has sold hundreds of thousands of copies (in hardback) around the world. I was as surprised by its success as anyone else, but its sales obviously reflected, and played a part in developing, the huge increase in interest in cigars that started around the same time as its publication. It was also – as an illustrated handbook and guide – very different from previous cigar books. I then wrote *The Essential Cigar*, a slim book aimed at beginners.

So why, you might ask, have I written *The Complete Cigar Book* ? The title says it all, really. The earlier books could only skirt many aspects of the subject; but there remains a great hunger for both information and guidance. So this time I wanted to put together as much cigar information in one small volume as possible. Very few cigar lovers, whether seasoned smokers or relative novices, could (in my opinion) want to know more about cigars and cigar smoking than the comprehensive facts, opinions and tips included in these covers. There is also a substantial history section and an anecdotal Who's Who of famous smokers – both of which, I hope, can be read for their inherent interest. There is even a tour of some of Havana's most famous bars. At your fingertips, then, is about as much information about cigars as most 'experts' know, me included. *The Complete Cigar Book* should answer all your questions, and should be the one cigar book you consult regularly.

The object, as with my earlier books, is to enhance your enjoyment, appreciation and knowledge of fine cigars. The book concentrates overwhelmingly on handmade cigars. I don't apologize for this: there is little of great interest to be written about machine-made cigars, enjoyable though they may be on occasions – though they are by no means ignored. Blame me for any errors (there will inevitably be some, despite my best endeavours).

Enjoy the book. Enjoy your cigars.

ANWER BATI
February 2000

CONTENTS

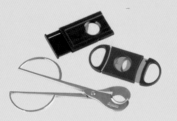

CIGAR PEOPLE
PAGE 219

CIGAR SUPPLIERS
PAGE 243

CIGARS
IN
HISTORY

A HISTORY
OF
CIGARS

Columbus, a non-smoker, arrives in the New World, 1492.

THE PRECISE ORIGIN of cigars is – to be frank – rather obscure. We don't know who smoked the first type of cigar, or precisely where. But we can be pretty confident that tobacco was first cultivated on the American continent, probably by the Maya of Central America, and most likely in the Yucatan peninsula.

A 10th-century piece of pottery discovered in Guatemala appears to show a Maya smoking a bundle of tobacco leaves tied with string, but since Mayan civilization had existed for over two thousand years by then, we really have no idea when tobacco was first smoked in this form. We also know that the Aztecs used to smoke a hollow reed filled with tobacco, and that other early inhabitants of Central and South America used to smoke crushed tobacco wrapped in vegetable leaves.

The native Americans of the north also smoked long pipes filled with tobacco, both for pleasure and as part of spiritual celebrations. So, at least we can be certain that tobacco has – one way or another – been smoked for many centuries, and certainly since the 10th century when a collapse in Mayan civilization led to migrations throughout the American continent – and quite possibly the spread of tobacco cultivation as a result.

COLUMBUS

However, tobacco wasn't known beyond America until Christopher Columbus's historic voyage of 1492 in an attempt to find a new route to India and China. Even then, exactly who actually introduced tobacco to Europe is a matter of some dispute.

Columbus landed in Cuba on 28th October, not quite sure where he was, but later recording that he thought it was China. Two of his men – Rodrigo de Jerez, and the linguist Luis de Torres – who were sent into the interior that November came back with reports that the people they encountered, the Taino Indians, " had torches in their hands and certain herbs to breathe in the smoke, dried herbs enclosed in a certain leaf, also dried... lit on one end, while on the other, they were drawing or sucking, breathing in that smoke, with which they numb their flesh and which is almost intoxicating, and in this way they say they never feel fatigue." And it is pretty likely that Rodrigo de Jerez was the first European to smoke these rudimentary cigars.

Later, Gonzalo Fernandez de Oviedo, in his *Natural History of the West Indies* (1535), recorded that: 'The Indians used a Y-shaped tube, putting the two ends of the fork up their nostrils and the tube in the burning grasses.' So, it would seem that tobacco was smoked in a variety of ways, and for medicinal and religious purposes (it was seen as a means of communing with the gods) as well as for pleasure. However, the true forerunner of the cigar consisted of twisted tobacco leaves rolled in a maize, palm or plantain leaf.

SIK'AR

It isn't obvious what the word 'tobacco', which the Taino were recorded as using, actually referred to. It could have been the leaf itself, the means of delivering the burning smoke, or the smoke itself, among other theories. Some suggest that the leaf was called *cohiba*, though it is also the case that the similar word *cojoba* referred to a form of snuff inhaled through a long pipe. As to the word cigar itself, its origin is probably the Mayan word *sik'ar*, the term for smoking – giving rise to the Spanish word *cigarro*. It is also possible that it derives from the word *jiq* or *ciq* – mentioned as a term for the cigar in the 16th-century Guatemalan Mayan text the *Popol Vuh*. Written in the Quiche language this chronicle of Mayan culture and history was discovered and translated into Spanish in the 18th century by the priest Francisco Jimenez. It has even been suggested that the word originated from *cigarra*, the Spanish word for cicada – a reference to the shape of the insect. Whatever its precise origins, the word *cigarro* was first noted in 1730, and its variant *seegar* first appeared in English dictionaries in 1735. But, once again, the early history of tobacco and cigars is far from clear-cut.

TOBACCO ARRIVES IN THE OLD WORLD

In the same way, we don't really know who first introduced tobacco to the Old World. Columbus himself was not particularly impressed by the custom of smoking, being more interested – as his letter to the King and Queen of Spain in 1494 makes clear – in gold. Sailors and explorers including the Florentine Amerigo Vespucci (after whom America was named), the monk, Ramon Pane, the Portuguese explorer Ferdinand Magellan (who certainly introduced tobacco to the Philippines) and his compatriot Alvarez Pedro Cabral, all have their supporters. Other claimants to the distinction include the conquistador Hernando Cortez, his fellow Spaniard Francisco Hernandez Goncalo, and Hernandez de Toledo, who is credited (by Portuguese sources, naturally) with planting tobacco seeds near Lisbon as early as 1520.

What we can be reasonably confident about is that, with much of the New World falling under European rule (the first colonial settlement in Cuba was founded in 1511), soon Spanish and other European sailors fell for the habit. They were followed by the conquistadors and colonists. In due course the returning conquistadors introduced tobacco and smoking to Spain and Portugal – some time around the middle of the 16th century.

Tobacco, a sign of wealth, then spread to France, credited in 1560 to the French ambassador to Portugal, Jean Nicot – though the priest André Thevet also has a claim to this distinction (in 1556, say his supporters). In any case, it was Nicot who eventually gave his name

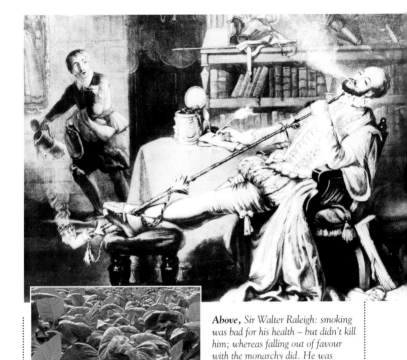

Above, *Sir Walter Raleigh: smoking was bad for his health – but didn't kill him; whereas falling out of favour with the monarchy did. He was executed in 1618.*

to nicotine, and *Nicotiana tabacum*, the Latin name for tobacco. It also spread to Italy. In Britain, as every schoolchild was once supposed to know, Sir Walter Ralegh was responsible for introducing tobacco. But now it is thought to have been one of Ralegh's men, Thomas Hariot, returning from a voyage on which Ralegh himself didn't go. It is true, though, that Ralegh helped to popularize smoking.

The plant was also used for medicinal purposes, famously by Catherine de Medici, Queen of France (introduced to it by Nicot), who took it in powdered form to alleviate her migraines; and it was taken by others to help soothe skin infections. It was known, at the time, as 'the Queen's herb' or, after Nicot started growing it, 'the Ambassador's herb'. Tobacco's medicinal qualities – it had been used for centuries in America to heal wounds, for instance – had been noted by a number of visitors to the New World, and word of its curative properties soon spread.

FULL-SCALE CULTIVATION

By the mid-16th century tobacco was well known in Europe, and by the beginning of the next century was already being cultivated by colonists in the Americas as a commercial crop to be traded with their countries of origin. Full-scale cultivation by European colonists started in Santo Domingo in 1531, in Cuba in 1580, and Brazil in 1600. Serious tobacco cultivation in Europe started in Portugal in 1558, in Spain the following year, in England in 1565, and in France in 1620.

Cuban tobacco plantation.

But despite its spreading fame, there were already those who wanted to ban its use, considering it an evil plant. Some of the denunciations of tobacco have a familiar ring to smokers today. In 1586, Philip II of Spain, for instance, ordered that growers and sellers of tobacco be whipped and threatened with exile, and that the plant 'be publicly burned as a harmful and damaging herb.' In Persia, Shah Abbas I condemned tobacco users to death; in 1645 Russia Czar Alexander ordered smokers to be deported to Siberia. In a bull of 1624, Pope Urban VIII threatened the citizens of Seville in particular, but smokers in general, with excommunication if they continued to smoke in church: 'feeling no shame, during the celebration of the very holy ordinance of the mass, soiling the sacred vestments with the repugnant humors that tobacco causes, infesting the temples with a repellent odour – to the great scandal of their brethren who keep to the righteous path...' And in England, in 1604, James I, in his famous *A Counterblast to Tobacco*, denounced smoking as an uncivilized pagan habit: 'A branch of the sin of drunkenness, which is the root of all sins… A custom loathsome to the eye, hateful to the nose, harmful to the brain, dangerous to the lungs, and in the black, stinking fume thereof, nearest resembling the horrible Stygian smoke of the pit that is bottomless.' It is, perhaps, no surprise that James imprisoned Sir Walter Raleigh in the Tower of London, or that he was executed in 1618.

Even Rodrigo de Jerez, probably the first European to try a cigar, was sent to jail during the previous century when he was found smoking in Ayamonte, in south-west Andalucia – when the smoke coming out of his mouth was misinterpreted as a case of demonic possession. To his satisfaction, however, when he was freed years later, he noticed that many of his neighbours had also started smoking.

Pipes and snuff

Apart from tobacco's medicinal applications, the way in which it was used tended to vary in different countries. In Britain (where tobacco shops had started opening by the end of the 17th century), France, The Netherlands and Germany, it was smoked in pipes and taken as snuff. In Spain and Portugal, however, it was smoked in a form resembling modern cigars. In any case, it was only used at this stage by the wealthy and those who had visited the New World.

In Spain, cigars using Cuban tobacco were made in Seville from 1676 onwards, with the royal factories of Seville being set up in 1731 – after a state monopoly on tobacco had been announced in 1717. The habit of smoking cigars (rather than using tobacco in other ways) gradually spread to other parts of Europe, so that before the end of the 18th century, cigar manufacture had moved north, with small factories being set up in Brittany in France, in Liege in Belgium, and in Germany.

Native Americans had, of course, smoked tobacco in pipe form for centuries, and this is the way American settlers originally used it, setting up the first colonial tobacco plantations in Virginia in 1612, and Maryland in 1631. The cigar itself probably first arrived in North America in 1762, when Colonel Israel Putnam returned from Cuba, where he had been an officer in the British army and took part in the siege and six-month British occupation of Havana. Putnam had been a farmer before fighting in the French and Indian Wars and came back to his home in Connecticut (an area where colonists had grown tobacco since the previous century) with bundles of Havana cigars and Cuban tobacco. Soon, cigar factories were set up in the Hartford area and tobacco was grown from Cuban seed. In 1775 Putnam gained another claim to fame by being appointed a major general in the Continental Army and fighting with distinction against the British at Bunker Hill in the American War of Independence.

Cuba

In Cuba, colonists started growing tobacco from the end of the 16th century, though by 1700 the population of the entire island numbered only 50,000. These *vegueros* waged a long-running battle against big landowners as exports of the crop grew. Some of them became tenant farmers; many others were forced to find new land to farm, opening up areas such as Oriente and Pinar del Río.

There were a number of rebellions (in 1717, 1721 and 1723) by *vegueros* against the Spanish monopoly (Estanco) on tobacco, the last of which was brutally repressed by the colonial authorities. At this stage, no cigars were actually made in Cuba. The monopoly obliged the farmers to sell tobacco – destined for Seville where processing and manufacture took place – solely to the government. Cuban growers finally started to make their own cigars on a small scale from the middle of the 18th century, but the vast majority of cigars were still made in Seville. By this time, the art of leaf growing,

Top, *Pinar del Río.* **Above** *and* **below,** *drying sheds.*

curing, fermentation and cigar making was gradually being perfected and refined. The idea of using different types of leaves for different parts of the cigar also evolved, and the present methods of making handmade cigars were fully developed by 1800 – so that the cigars available at the time were recognizably similar to those we smoke today. Such was the growing demand for cigars that, at the turn of the 19th century, more than 5,000 people worked in the cigar factories of Spain. By then, cigars had started to be manufactured throughout the rest of Europe, particularly in The Netherlands, which was able to import suitable tobacco from its Far Eastern and other colonies.

CIGARS IN VOGUE

The first Englishman recorded as smoking a cigar was John Cockburn, who did so in Honduras in 1731, but cigar smoking didn't really take off in France and Britain until after the Peninsular War (1808-14) when a coalition of the British, Spanish and Portuguese forces fought against Napoleon's armies in the Iberian Peninsula. The returning French and British veterans subsequently spread to their home countries the habit they had learned while serving in Spain and Portugal. By the early 19th century, snuff had become the main way of taking tobacco, replacing the pipe. But now cigars started to take off as the smart new fashion in Britain. In 1823, some 15,000 cigars were imported by the British. That figure had surged to 13 million by 1840. The first major consignment of Cuban cigars to arrive in Britain was in 1830, stocked by the famous Robert Lewis shop – a tobacconist since 1787, and still open today. Production of segars or seegars, as they were then called, began in Britain in 1820, though an Act of Parliament was soon passed to set out regulations governing production. A new import tax also ensured that foreign cigars in Britain remained a luxury item, confined to the wealthy.

As demand for cigars rose, so did the call for better quality and the Sevillas, as Spanish cigars were called (the Spanish themselves called them *puros*), were gradually superseded by those from Cuba. The reason was simple: it had been observed that finished cigars weathered the long voyage from Cuba much better than tobacco leaf. This fact resulted in an eventual decline of the Spanish cigar industry, and a rapid growth in the production of Havanas. Cuba was still a Spanish colony and a decree by King Ferdinand VII of Spain in 1821 set out to encourage the production of Cuban cigars by relaxing Spanish controls on the sale and production of tobacco. The change also provided a useful new source of tax revenue for Spain, an irresistible and highly lucrative consideration for governments which (along with state monopolies, Seita in France, for instance) has gone hand in hand with the production and sale of tobacco products to this day.

Home of the Cohiba: Havana's El Laguito factory, housed in a grand Italianate mansion.

By the mid-19th century, there were 9,500 plantations, and numerous factories in Havana and other cities started springing up (there were as many as 1,300, at one stage, though this

Sign outside the Partagas factory, one of Havana's key tourist attractions.

number had shrunk to around 120 by the beginning of the 20th century), and cigar production became a major Cuban industry. Export was mainly to the United States until tariff barriers were raised in 1857. The very first trademarks to be registered were by Bernardino Rencurrel and H. de Cabanas y Carbajal in 1810, but the first of the great brands to be introduced was Partagas in 1827. As trade grew, brand and size differentiation – and marketing generally – became important, and by the middle of the century, cedar cigar boxes with logos or labels (introduced by H. Upmann in the 1840s), and bands (the invention of Dutchman Gustave Bock in 1850) had become a feature of cigar salesmanship. It was the beginning of the modern world of cigars.

By the early 19th century, Cuban cigars were being exported to the United States – and domestic production was also taking off, with the first American cigar factory set up in Connecticut in 1810, and others founded in Pennsylvania and New York. Today Connecticut tobacco provides some of the best wrapper leaves to be found outside Cuba; local cultivation of the leaves started there in the 1820s.

Although John Quincy Adams, sixth President of the United States, was a keen cigar smoker (it is probable that he was introduced to cigars during his time as a diplomat in The Netherlands, France and England), cigar smoking didn't really become a widespread habit in the United States until the time of the Civil War. General (later 18th President) Ulysses S. Grant was a notable devotee often pictured with a cigar in hand or mouth. Other American luminaries of the early to mid-19th century, including fourth President James Madison, seventh President Andrew Jackson and 12th President General Zachary Taylor, commander of the victorious American forces in the Mexican-American War, are also known to have smoked cigars. It is a habit continued to the present day by many of their successors both illustrious and, in more recent times, controversial.

Right, *a selection of classic brands.*

HAVANA, A HOUSEHOLD NAME

By the time of the Civil War (1861-65), the word Havana had
become a generic term, and the name given to the most expensive
American cigars, made with Cuban tobacco and five times the price
of the regular domestic product. Some of the best known domestic
cigars came from the factory at Conestoga, Pennsylvania, which gave
its name to the 'stogie' (a term first noted in 1853). Many domestic
cigars used American binders and wrappers and Cuban filler leaves
(frequently blended with domestic filler) at this stage. By the late
19th century, the cigar had become a status symbol in the United
States. A tax decrease in the 1870s made the cigar even more popular
and widely available, and encouraged domestic production. Today,
the United States is the world's biggest cigar market.

Cigar smoking became such a regular pastime for fashionable
gentlemen in Britain and France that smoking cars became a feature
of European trains, cigar 'divans' opened and the smoking room was
introduced in hotels and gentlemen's clubs. In Britain, by the late
19th century, the custom of smoking cigars with port or brandy when
the ladies withdrew to another room after dinner had become an
established social convention amongst the upper and upper-middle
classes. The habit even influenced clothing, with the advent of the
smoking jacket to keep clothes free of the lingering smell of cigars. In
France, black tie wear (the tuxedo) is still referred to as Le Smoking.

*The Prince of Wales,
future Edward VII,
around 1870: one of
the all-time great
cigar enthusiasts.*

The fashion for cigars was given a major boost by the fact that the Prince of Wales (the future Edward VII), was a devotee, much to the chagrin of his mother, Queen Victoria, who was not amused by the habit. At the beginning of his nine-year reign in 1901, he famously announced, after one of his first official dinners: "Gentlemen, you may smoke."

In America, by 1920, Thomas Marshall, Woodrow Wilson's Vice President, was reported as saying: "What this country really needs is a good five-cent cigar," an ambition not to be achieved until more than 30 years later when new methods of cigar production allowed truly cheap cigars to be made by machine. At around the same time, the columnist and poet F.P. Adams, sneered in verse in *The Rich Man*:

> *The rich man in his motor car,*
> *His country and his town estate.*
> *He smokes a fifty-cent cigar*
> *And jeers at Fate.*

The envy provoked in some by fine cigars and the popular image of their smokers was clearly taking shape.

Competition from the cigarette

Cigar consumption in the United States peaked in 1907, gradually falling due to the increasing popularity of the more democratic cigarette. The cigarette, or 'paper cigar' was first 'invented' when paupers in Seville started to pick up discarded cigar butts, shredded them, and rolled the tobacco in pieces of paper. Those working in Seville's cigar factories did the same with leftover scraps of tobacco. But cigarette smoking didn't become widespread until the early 19th century, when it started to become common in Spain, France and Italy (and, by the mid-19th century, in Greece, Turkey and Russia). The habit didn't really become popular in Britain until after the Crimean War, when it was brought back from Russia by returning soldiers. But it was the introduction of cigarette-making machines in the 1880s that really accelerated the spread of this form of smoking – and the eventual demise of cigars as the main way of taking tobacco.

In Cuba, on the other hand, the cigar had become a national symbol, partly because, as the industry grew, cigar makers became key members of the Cuban industrial working class – with tobacco the second biggest export product after sugar. They even established the unique custom – which continues to this day – of rollers reading literary, political and other texts, including the works of Dumas, Zola and Victor Hugo to their colleagues to alleviate boredom and encourage education. One of these books was *The Count of Monte Cristo*, later the name of one of the great Havana brands.

Below, boxing cigars.

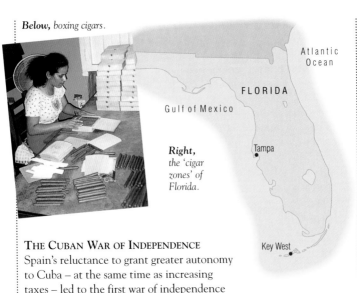

Right,
the 'cigar
zones' of
Florida.

THE CUBAN WAR OF INDEPENDENCE

Spain's reluctance to grant greater autonomy
to Cuba – at the same time as increasing
taxes – led to the first war of independence
from the colonial power (1868-78), and another war in 1895 during
which civilians were killed by both sides, and towns and plantations
burned. By 1898, commercial activity had virtually ground to a halt.
As a result, during the mid to late 19th century, many cigar workers
emigrated to Florida to escape poverty and the political turmoil on
Cuba, eventually setting up cigar industries in their new country in
towns such as Tampa and Key West. Such was the scale of
immigration that at the end of the 19th century 12,000 of the 18,000
workers in Key West were Cubans, mostly employed in the tobacco
industry. Many other rollers and growers migrated to the Dominican
Republic, Honduras, Jamaica, Mexico and Venezuela.

Significantly, these Cubans abroad helped to fund the final revolt
against Spain, led in 1895 by José Martí, the Cuban national hero.
Given their part in the struggle, tobacco workers in Cuba began to
play an important part in national and political life. Even Marti's
order for the uprising was, symbolically, sent from Key West to Cuba
concealed in a cigar.

During the early years of the 20th century, Cuba was first under the
direct, and then indirect, control of the United States, and started to
recover economically. Innovations were attempted, such as the
machine production of cigars in the 1920s. In Cuba, the firm of Por
Larranaga was in the forefront of this development – to much initial
opposition from its workers. Machine production in the United States
also started, resulting in the fact that machine-made cigars rose from
10 per cent of total cigar production in 1924, to a huge 98 per cent by
the 1950s.

Castro, leader of the Cuban revolution, lights up. He gave up smoking in the early 1990s.

CASTRO

Cigar workers continued to be in the mainstream of political awareness after Fidel Castro's revolution against General Batista in 1959 – not least because Cubans of African extraction, descendants of former slaves, and many of them in the tobacco industry, had until then been excluded in the main from political power. The cigar was also a symbol of Castro's revolution, quite apart from El Commandante's own fondness for smoking. When he was a prisoner he was sent messages hidden in his cigars. Ironically, though, he gave up a few years ago – ostensibly to set a healthy example to his countrymen.

After Castro started to nationalize Cuban and foreign assets, the United States embargo on Cuba, imposed in 1962, meant that Havana cigars could no longer be legally imported into the U.S., apart from in small quantities for personal use. A very significant blow, when you consider that the Tobacco Trust had, at one stage early in the 20th century, imported no fewer than 291 cigar brands into the United States, keeping standards high and allowing the Cubans to export some 250 million cigars a year – though this figure had fallen to only 44 million a couple of years before Castro's revolution. The cigar industry – much of which was American owned before Castro – was nationalized along with everything else, and henceforth run by the state monopoly, Cubatabaco.

EXODUS

A number of the leading cigar factory owners such as the Menendez, Palicio and Cifuentes families left Cuba, resolving to set up their businesses again, often using the names of the Havana brands they had owned before the revolution. That is why cigars called Partagas, Romeo Y Julieta and H. Upmann are made in the Dominican Republic, and Punch and Hoyo de Monterrey come from Honduras – often with logos almost indistinguishable from their Havana namesakes. These brands are similar to their Cuban counterparts in name and packaging only, even though they are often good cigars in their own right. The dispossessed former factory owners of Cuba, and those who followed in their wake, also started making entirely new brands – to such effect that the Dominican Republic today, after development by ex-Cuban and American companies over almost three decades, produces over half of the handmade cigars imported into the United States, and many of the finest cigars in the world outside Cuba. Even the famous Davidoff brand withdrew from Cuba in 1990, switching to production in the Dominican Republic after a dispute with the Cuban government.

Honduras has also become a major supplier to the American and other important markets.

Partagas Limited Reserve Royale

Romeo Y Julieta Churchill

H.Upmann Corona

Punch Presidente

Hoyo de Monterrey Governor

Davidoff Tubo No .2

COHIBA

Habana, Cuba

Habanos s.a.

Left, Cohiba was created to help maintain Cuba's reputation after the Castro revolution. Below, roller at work.

As for Cuba itself, many claimed that cigar quality fell after the revolution (pre-revolutionary cigars have become collectors' items), a charge understandably refuted by the Cubans, who responded by creating the Cohiba brand in 1966, designed at the time to be the best cigar available by any standards. But the criticism was not wholly without foundation: some of Cuba's finest cigar makers had, after all, fled abroad, and there was considerable financial pressure on the Cubans to cut corners on production. There was also a revolution in Cuban cigar factories themselves – with women starting to roll cigars in the early 1960s. Until then, only men did this key task and women were confined to selecting leaves (sometimes sorting them on their thighs – thus giving rise to the famous myth about cigars being rolled on the thighs of Cuban maidens).

Cigars, of course, have always been associated with the wealthy and powerful in the public imagination, and the communist Cubans initially found this irony surrounding their most famous export embarrassing. At one stage, soon after the revolution, some even wanted to abolish brands and create a single 'Peoples' Cigar'. But, luckily for the rest of the world, financial necessity, with the collapse of European communism and the disappearance of the support the Cuban economy enjoyed for 30 years from the former Eastern Bloc, meant that the cigar industry attained a new importance – as an obvious way of accumulating much-needed foreign exchange.

RATIONALIZATION

In 1979, the Cubans rationalized the industry, standardizing sizes and cutting down the number of brands they produced. Cuban cigar factories today all produce more than one brand, some specializing in particular sizes, others in particular flavours. Some observers believe that standards fell as a result of these changes, though more recently – conscious that quality is the only serious advantage Cuban cigars have over their competitors – efforts have been made to keep standards high and consistent. Another rationalization took place in 1993. But by the end of the 1990s, the Cubans had actually started introducing new brands, and boosted tobacco acreage to cope with the rising demand for their handmade cigars. At the time of writing, Cuba exports well over 100 million handmade cigars a year, compared with only 30 million just after the revolution.

Over the last few years, trademark battles have taken place between the Cubans and manufacturers elsewhere – mostly American-owned companies using the same brand names. These have included legendary brands such as Montecristo and Cohiba. And it is very likely that if Cuban cigars are finally allowed to be imported into the United States, there will be a bonanza for lawyers, as other brand owners slug it out with the Cubans.

These legal battles, of course, only serve to emphasize the boom in cigar smoking in general, and premium cigars in particular, in the 1990s. It can be dated back to 1993 after the launch of the magazine *Cigar Aficionado* in September of the previous year and, if I may say so rather immodestly, the publication of books such as my best-selling *The Cigar Companion*.

This page, *the popular U.S. cigar magazine that rode on the 1990s cigar boom;* **opposite,** *cigars awaiting auction at Christie's, the London auction house.*

Dream load: a shipment of Montecristo No. 4 leaves Partagas's factory for the warehouse.

What were the reasons? The fact that cigars are safer than cigarettes can't be ruled out, but a more likely reason is the fact that the economies of, for instance, the United States, the United Kingdom, France and Germany were all either growing or recovering from recession by the mid-1990s, allowing extra disposable income to be spent on luxuries (necessities some would say) such as cigars. There was also a carry-over from the 1980s boom in some of these countries – allowing those who had made good in that decade to spend freely on status symbols without fear of embarrassment. This applied particularly in the United States (and to some extent in Britain) where the Dow Jones index had risen from 780 in August 1982 to stand at over 11,000 by May 1999.

Whatever the precise combination of reasons, it is undeniable that they, along with increasing knowledge of handmade cigars and vigorous marketing by those in the trade, made premium cigar sales soar, with an estimated number of over 100,000 new cigar smokers in the United States in 1994. The number of premium cigars imported into the United States rose from 107 million in 1993, to 126 million in 1994. By 1995 the number of imported premium cigars had risen by a further 31 per cent. And by 1996, 297 million premium cigars were exported to the U.S. – rising to a staggering 500 million by 1997. Premium cigar sales also rose in Europe, and in the wealthier nations of South East Asia – though not quite so fast – with steady growth in the market (a 16 per cent increase in 1997 in Britain, for instance). Having said that, total U.S. cigar sales (including machine-mades) stand at around 3-3.5 billion at the time of writing, as opposed to 9 billion in 1970.

One reflection of the fact that premium cigars had become fashionable again was that the age profile of cigar smokers, particularly in the United States, also became significantly lower during the 1990s.

The fastest-growing part of the handmade cigar market in the early 1990s was represented by young Americans typically aged between 26 and 38.

Above, the second-floor bar at The Havana Club and Monte's; **right,** the Churchill Bar with its cigar divan – two of London's cigar-friendly places. **Opposite:** European counterparts to Cigar Aficionado.

CIGAR FEVER

The new vogue for cigars has had many other side-effects: the growth of cigar clubs, cigar events and cigar-friendly restaurants, for instance. A number of new cigar magazines have sprung up around the world – in Spain, France (*Amateur de Cigare*) and Austria, as well as in the United States – and numerous new books have been published, when once only a handful existed. Cigars are also now regularly covered in newspapers and general interest magazines; and TV films (such as a BBC programme broadcast at Christmas, 1998) have documented the boom. The Internet has also had its part to play: by the late 1990s, dozens of cigar-related websites were flourishing, as well as on-line cigar magazines. Even the horse, owned by Allen Paulson, that dominated the American 1995 and 1996 racing seasons was a colt called Cigar. But a less welcome consequence of this florescence of cigar culture is the major increase in the number of fake Havanas which have appeared around the world.

Around the middle of 1997 there were signs that the cigar boom was levelling out – at least in the short term. At the time of writing there are an estimated 100 million unsold handmade cigars in the United States. One of the reasons for this glut is the appearance on the market of what have become contemptuously known in the industry as Don Nobodies – cheap handmades, not properly matured, which suddenly appeared to meet demand created by inexperienced smokers and as a result undercut established brands. Another reason is that, as a result of shortages in the mid-1990s (larger sizes were particularly difficult to come by), many dedicated smokers started stocking up heavily when production, particularly in the Dominican Republic, was eventually increased. Those stocks will take some time to be smoked. As a result of this surplus, prices at the bottom end of the handmade market fell. And the profits and share prices of large U.S. manufacturers such as General Cigar and Consolidated Cigar (the biggest U.S. cigar company) also took a dive, with a reduction of net profits from $13 million to $10 million reported by Consolidated Cigar for the second quarter of 1998, for instance.

Above: *if you visit Cuba, don't be tempted by cigars, apparently with famous names, offered on the streets – they're fakes. This enthusiast knows better: he organizes guided cigar trips to Havana.*
Opposite: *if you're visiting Cuba and see a local smoking a cigar, it will be 'domestic', not Havana. All the best hand-mades are reserved for export.*

The cigar boom – however long it lasts – has benefited many countries other than those mentioned above. Increased investment means that Costa Rica is now a source of decent leaf, and Ecuador has begun to produce good wrapper tobacco. Countries such as Jamaica, Brazil, Mexico, and Nicaragua all have old cigar making traditions, but now their leaf is also in demand from manufacturers elsewhere: Mexican binder tobacco is currently widely used by a number of major premium brands. It remains to be seen, however, how the devastation caused by Hurricane Mitch in 1998 will affect production in Honduras and Nicaragua in the long term. Further afield, Cameroon in West Africa produces some of the finest dark wrapper leaves in the world, and the Indonesian islands of Java and Sumatra, which have old links with the cigar industries of The Netherlands, Switzerland and Germany (for machine-mades) are now also important as suppliers of wrapper leaf to New World producers. In the same way, the Philippines and the Canary Islands, historically linked to Spain, produce leaf used by a number of manufacturers, as well as their own cigars.

WOMEN AND CIGARS

A much-hyped collateral result of the cigar boom is that it has become chic for women to smoke premium cigars. The trend was led by supermodels and films stars such as Claudia Schiffer, Linda Evangelista, Sharon Stone, Whoopi Goldberg, Drew Barrymore and Demi Moore – many of whom have been featured on the covers of magazines such as Cigar Aficionado *and* Smoke, *as well as being pictured with stogies in their mouths at film premières and cigar events.*

Women have smoked cigars in Cuba, South and Central America, and Spain ever since modern cigars were first manufactured, though never to the same extent as men. They have also done so in other countries since the 19th century. Most famously, 1930s Berlin had a number of women-only cigar clubs. But in Europe, until recently, women (such as George Sand, Colette, Marlene Dietrich and Virginia Woolf) who smoked cigars were seen as either making a point about their sexuality or challenging the male establishment – particularly during an era when, remember, women would traditionally withdraw after dinner to let the men smoke.

Opposite, *Whoopi Goldberg;* **above,** *Marlene Dietrich.*

Cigar smoking was regarded as an almost exclusively male activity, thought to be positively unpleasant for women. 'I do not believe that there was ever an Aunt Tabithy who could abide cigars,' wrote Donald G. Mitchell in his *Reveries of a Bachelor* in 1850. In the same vein, C.B. Hartley, in *The Gentleman's Book of Etiquette* (1873), advised: 'Do not smoke in the street until after dark, and then remove your cigar from your mouth if you meet a lady.'

In 1845, when George Sand lit up a large cigar in front of a young Russian aristocrat, she responded to his amazement at the fact that she was smoking, by saying: "In St.Petersburg I probably would not be able to smoke a cigar in a salon." To which he supposedly replied: "In no salon, Madame, have I ever seen a woman smoking a cigar."

So just why have large numbers of women started smoking cigars over the last few years? It could, of course, be just a matter of jumping on the bandwagon, with cigars being nothing more than the latest fashion accessory. Or perhaps women now smoke cigars for the same reason many men have smoked them for the past 150 years: to assert power, wealth and prestige – as symbolized by the poster for the film *The First Wives Club*, where Goldie Hawn, Bette Midler and Diane Keaton were pictured with fat cigars, celebrating victory over their husbands.

Opposite, Harrods' cigar department and its manager. Right, girl power, Havana-style.

Ironically, it seems that the anti-smoking lobby in America may be responsible for the growth of cigar chic, partly because cigars are much healthier than cigarettes and partly because of their new cachet both socially and in the media. Nobody, after all, is writing glossy magazine articles celebrating women smoking cigarettes.

But speculation apart, the trend seems to be a genuine one and more women – mostly highly-paid professionals – are certainly smoking cigars today than in the past. In America, it is thought that over 200,000 cigars a year are sold to women. And special, women-only, cigar clubs, lunches and dinners are now common. In Britain, according to the owner of one cigar retailer, "once we were used to women buying cigars for their boyfriends, but now more are buying them for themselves." In Europe, women tend to go for smaller sizes, but American women, on the other hand, seem willing to match men for the larger 'power' sizes.

Women's attitude to cigars seems to be different from the male approach. Women, for a start, are more willing to ask for advice than men. "The difficulty with guys," says Simon Chase of British importers Hunters and Frankau, "is that they think they know it all. They're embarrassed to ask questions. But women like to be told how to smoke and what to choose."

Women are also playing an increasingly important role in the cigar trade. In 1998, for instance, *Cigar Aficionado* ran a feature about eight women who had broken into the previously very male world of cigar retailing. And in 1999, Jean Clark, manager of the cigar department of Harrods department store, in London, was nominated as one of the world's top five Havana retailers by the Cubans.

CIGARS IN ART

Sigmund Freud.

*Cigar smokers and cigar making have been subjects which
have fascinated many artists over the centuries.
At first it was simply a matter of curiosity:
the urge to record a new fashion and a fascination
with the mysteries of cigar smoking and manufacture.
But later cigars became a feature of portraits of famous
smokers, and also provided a useful prop for the sitter.*

THE FIRST KNOWN European illustration of 'cigars' being smoked by Indians was a woodcut produced in 1557 by André Thevet, a French priest who had visited Brazil, and subsequently wrote about the tobacco plant. Some claim he introduced the plant to France. Thevet also featured an illustration of a tobacco plant in his book *Universal Cosmography*.

Any number of Dutch and Flemish paintings of the 17th century show people smoking clay pipes, but once cigar manufacture began in Europe the work of some of the new factories also started appearing in paintings (a series of scenes from the Liege factory by the 18th-century Belgian artist Leonard Defrance, for instance) and in illustrations for books such as Denis Diderot's *Encyclopédie* in France. The French printmaker Gustave Dore also illustrated the royal tobacco factories of Seville in 1866.

By the mid-19th century, by which time cigar smoking was fashionable in both Europe and the United States, paintings of the wealthy, famous and modish often depicted them with cigars (though, it must be said, the poor continued to be shown smoking pipes). The portrait of an Italian dandy by Domenico Morelli, or Toulouse-Lautrec's 1891 painting of Louis Pascal, are examples. Writers and artists, too, had taken up the habit, and cigar smoking was seen as a sign of being 'artistic'. Thus, the French poet Stephane Mallarme, co-founder of the Symbolist movement, was painted with a cigar in his hand by both Edouard Manet and François Nardi. Mallarme's fellow poet and critic Charles Baudelaire, author of *Les Fleurs du mal* was also pictured with a cigar (by Charles Ney). Artists' studios also became a popular subject for group portraits – with some of those gathered occasionally smoking or holding cigars. Spanish and Cuban painters, naturally, paid more attention to cigars than those of northern Europe: the work of the Basque artist Victor Patricio Landaluze (such as *The Healer*, showing an old woman smoking a cigar, and *The Apprentice*, portraying a young cigar maker).

Goya's once sensational *Naked Maja*, painted at the beginning of the 19th century, has a place in cigar history, too. It was originally thought to be a depiction of his mistress, the Duchess of Alba, but it is now suspected that Goya's real model was a female cigar worker. But when women were actually shown smoking cigars in the 19th and early 20th century, it was inevitably to indicate either their dubious morals or their ambivalent sexuality.

Archetypal scene in a Victorian smoking room – an illustration published in Punch *magazine, 1886.*

Cartoons, in a similar way, used the cigar to indicate wealth or rapaciousness – and sometimes still do. The stereotyped caricature of the capitalist cigar smoker started early in the United States and Britain, particularly in the left-wing press: though not, for obvious – if paradoxical – reasons, in communist Cuba.

Amongst modern artists, keen cigar smokers included Picasso, the surrealist Marcel Duchamp and the Dutch-born Fauvist painter Kees Van Dongen, (who once wrote: 'The cigar, like the pipe, ought to match your physique'). Raoul Dufy even used to exchange his paintings for cigars. Others such as the Mexican painter Diego Rivera (his 1916 *Still Life with Cigar*, for instance), René Magritte, Man Ray (in etchings portraying Duchamp) and Larry Rivers (his 1964 *Dutch Masters and Cigars* series) have featured cigars in their work. They have also been the subject of a number of canvases by artists in the 1990s. Recently Frank Stella, a cigar lover, has used the movement and patterns created by cigar smoke as the basis for some of his work.

Photographers, of course, have been taking portraits of the famous with cigars from Matthew Brady in the American Civil War (notably General Grant) onwards – including such noted smokers as the great British engineer Isambard Kingdom Brunel (as early as 1857), Edward VII, Sigmund Freud, Thomas Mann, Evelyn Waugh, Count Basie, John F. Kennedy and any number of movie stars from Charlie Chaplin and Groucho Marx to Jack Nicholson and Arnold Schwarzenegger.

Churchill in familiar bulldog pose, abetted by cigar.

Cigars, as photographers discovered, are a useful prop – and help to relax the subject. But one of the most memorable portraits of a great smoker – Yousuf Karsh's 1941 photograph of Winston Churchill – shows him without his customary cigar. The growling Churchill, looking at his most defiant, was actually deprived of his smoke by Karsh, who recalled: 'Churchill's cigar was ever present. I held out an ashtray, but he would not dispose of it....Then I stepped towards him and, without premeditation, but ever so respectfully, I said, "forgive me, sir" and plucked the cigar out of his mouth. By the time I got back to my camera, he looked so belligerent he could have devoured me.'

CIGARS IN LITERATURE

Victor Hugo.

The earliest references to cigars tended,
as one might expect, to occur in the memoirs and journals
of travellers and others who encountered them in Cuba
and other parts of the New World.
The first of these accounts were the reports of
Luis de Torres and Rodrigo de Jerez's encounters
with the Taino Indians in Cuba in 1492.
These were followed by, amongst others,
the Englishman John Cockburn's description (1735)
of cigar smoking by both men and women in
Honduras and Costa Rica.

Stephane Mallarme.

THE 18TH-CENTURY French social reformer, the Duc de La Rochefoucauld, who was sent to liaise with the American revolutionary government in 1794, wrote of cigars in his account of his voyage. 'The cigar is a great resource,' he said, '.... It raises your spirits.'

The Briton, Sir Charles Murray, in his book *Visit to Cuba*, published in 1836, was equally effusive, describing cigars which had been sent back to Havana from England as 'the most delicious cigars that even a meditative philosopher could have dreamed.'

One of the earliest major works to mention cigars was Giacomo Casanova's autobiography, describing his adventures travelling through 18th-century Europe (though first published in 1826, almost 30 years after the death of the great libertine).

French writers of the 19th century frequently mentioned cigars in their work – the novelist Stendhal (author of *The Red and the Black*), for instance. His compatriot, the poet Auguste Barthélmy wrote a *Manual on the Art of Smoking* in 1849 – in 5,000 Alexandrine verses including: 'For the man who is not a hapless layman, 'neath the firmament nothing surpasses the Havana cigar.' Victor Hugo, the great French novelist described tobacco as 'the plant that converts thoughts into dreams.' Stephane Mallarme was introduced to cigars by his father – and wrote about his love for them. And the poet and playwright Alfred de Musset took the view that 'Any cigar smoker is a friend, because I know what he feels.'

Some female French writers, such as George Sand, were cigar lovers. She wrote: 'Cigars calm pain and people loneliness with a thousand gracious images.' She was also the lover of Chopin, Alfred de Musset (who once wrote a poem describing Sand smoking a cigar) and Prosper Mérimée, author of Carmen – set in a Seville tobacco factory. Before she became an established writer, Sand used to supplement her income by embellishing cigar boxes with water colour designs. Her successor as one of France's leading women writers, Colette (who died in 1954) referred to cigars in Gigi. The character Aunt Alice says in the novel: "Let me think how I will teach you to choose cigars...when a woman knows a man's preferences, cigars included, and when a man knows what pleases a woman, they are well armed for life together."

Among British writers who praised cigars were the historian Thomas Carlyle (1785-1881), who advocated the introduction of cigar smoking to Parliament to calm debate. (Not a bad idea: cigar smoking was, after all, once allowed in the U.S. Congress.) And the Victorian poet, critic and politician Edward Bulwer-Lytton (later Lord Lytton) wrote, in 1845: 'A good cigar is as great a comfort to a man as a good cry to a woman.' Lord Byron, actually wrote an ode, *Sublime Tobacco*, in *The Island*, which ends with the lines:

> *Yet thy true lovers more adore by far*
> *Thy naked beauties – Give me a cigar!*

The poet Thomas Hood also celebrated cigars in verse (in a poem, unimaginatively, perhaps, entitled *The Cigar*, written around 1840).

Many of the greatest British novelists of the Victorian era were not only keen cigar smokers themselves, but wrote about cigars in their work. They included Dickens, Trollope (a photograph of him smoking a cigar exists) and, above all, perhaps, Thackeray. Thackeray not only wrote about the pleasures of cigar smoking ('...one of the greatest creature comforts of my life...') but found that cigars helped him to write. There are a number of references to cigars in his great novel – set in the Napoleonic period – *Vanity Fair* (1847). It includes a scene in which the feisty heroine, the adventuress Becky Sharp, briefly smokes after the lumbering dragoon, Captain Crawley, asks her whether she minds his cigar. He needn't have worried. As Thackeray writes: 'Miss Sharp loved the smell of a cigar out of doors beyond everything in the world...' Becky goes on to marry Crawley later in the novel.

The Nobel Prize-winning poet and novelist of the British Empire, Rudyard Kipling was a cigar lover who – in *The Betrothed* (1886) – came out with the line, now notorious, 'A woman is only a woman, but a good cigar is a smoke.' Kipling has been much maligned as a

Above, *Rudyard Kipling.*

Henry Clay Breva

misogynist for this line by those who don't know the poem in full or its context. This is grossly unfair. In fact, the poem, about choosing between a woman, Maggie, and smoking, is in fact satirical. It was inspired by a breach of promise case brought in the British courts in 1885 – during which it was alleged that the husband preferred cigars to his wife. As a poet, Kipling was merely trying to enter the mind of the husband in the case. *The Betrothed* mentions a number of Havana brands such as Larranaga, Partagas and Henry Clay, and demonstrates a considerable knowledge of cigars.

H.G. Wells describes the eponymous hero of *The Invisible Man* (1897) demanding a cigar after dinner and biting the end off before a knife could be produced. The character refers to "This blessed gift of smoking!"

The novelist and short story writer Somerset Maugham (1874-1965), author of *Liza of Lambeth*, *The Moon and Sixpence* and *Of Human Bondage*, wrote in his autobiography *The Summing Up*: 'A good cigar is one of the best pleasures that I know. At the time when I was young and very poor, I only smoked cigars which were offered to me. I promised myself that if I ever had some money that I would savour a cigar each day after lunch and after dinner. This is the only resolution of my youth that I have kept, and the only realized ambition which has not brought disillusion.'

Partagas Corona

Maugham's contemporary, the novelist and critic Virginia Woolf, was a founder member of the famous Bloomsbury Group, which believed in free living – and Woolf extended her credo to the smoking of cigars.

Evelyn Waugh (1903-1966), perhaps the leading British novelist of the 20th century, certainly of his generation, was an enthusiastic cigar smoker and bon vivant. The Partagas brand was mentioned in his greatest work, *Brideshead Revisited*, and his diary contains many references to cigar smoking.

Cigars have featured in the work of many great American writers. They are mentioned, for instance, in Stephen Crane's *Red Badge of Courage* – set in the American Civil War. Later, Ernest Hemingway, who lived in Cuba (there are many Cuban locations in his work), and was a great devotee of cigars, wrote about them in novels such as *The Old Man and the Sea* and *The Sun Also Rises* (originally called *Fiesta*). In the latter, one character, the Count, says: "I like a cigar to really draw...Half the cigars you smoke don't draw."

But perhaps the keenest lover of cigars in the whole of American literature was Mark Twain. Twain, who wrote about cigars in his autobiography, and even had a brand named after him, was precocious: he started smoking at the age

Mark Twain.

of eight. When he wrote he would typically smoke 15 to 20 cheap cigars a day. In 1871, shortly after getting married, he moved to Hartford, Connecticut, a leading centre of cigar production. He once said: "If cigar smoking is not permitted in Heaven, I won't go."

The legendary American journalist, critic and social commentator, H.L. Mencken, was almost as keen on cigars as Twain. He started smoking them aged 16, but then cigars were, more or less, in his blood. His father, August Mencken, was owner of a major Baltimore cigar factory, and fully expected his son – who actually learned to roll cigars – to follow him into the business.

Che Guevara.

Many Cuban and Spanish writers have, for obvious historical and cultural reasons, written about cigars. They include the major 20th-century Spanish poet and playwright Frederico Garcia Lorca, who evoked the colourful lithographs decorating the boxes of the Fonseca and Romeo Y Julieta brands in a poem. And, more recently, the Cuban novelist, short-story writer and diplomat Guillermo Cabrera Infante (who eventually left Cuba to live in London) wrote his famous book of vignettes featuring cigars, *Holy Smoke* (1985).

Romeo Y Julieta box lithograph.

HABANA

HABANA · CUBA

– 48 –

José Martí, the Cuban revolutionary who led the revolt against Spain in 1895, was also an important poet and essayist. He once wrote of tobacco that it was the 'comfort of the pensive, delight of the daydreamer...' The Argentine-born revolutionary Che Guevara was also very fond of cigars, and often mentioned them in his writings about guerilla warfare and in his diaries. He once said : 'An habitual and extremely important complement in the life of a guerilla is smoking ...'

Famous writers with a fondness for smoking cigars from countries not so obviously connected with them have included Thomas Mann, the German author of *Buddenbrooks* and *The Magic Mountain*. Mann has a character (Hans Castort) in the latter book saying: "I fail to understand how one can live without smoking. It means, undoubtedly, depriving oneself of the best part of existence and, in any case, a very considerable pleasure..." One of Russia's greatest novelists, Fyodor Dostoyevsky, in *The Idiot* (1868, published in English in 1887) describes an incident in a train carriage featuring the displeasure of two ladies in a first-class carriage when a cigar is smoked. One of them grabs it and throws it out of the window – prompting the smoker to do the same to her lapdog. Not, perhaps, the best demonstration of good manners shown by a smoker, but not a great advertisement for those who object either.

Such unfortunate incidents apart, however, most references to cigars by major writers over the years have been in to evoke pleasure, relaxation, contemplation and savoir faire. Occasionally, they have been used to indicate vulgarity or brashness: but not remotely as often as they have been used to symbolize these traits in cartoons or films. The most obvious reason is that so many fine writers have found cigar smoking conducive to productivity.

Fonseca box lithograph.

CIGARS
IN THE MOVIES

Danny DeVito.

Cigars have appeared in films from early silents onwards. In the twenties, thirties and forties their presence partly reflected the fact that they were widely smoked – particularly in America. But they have also served a number of symbolic purposes – in much the same way they have in cartoons and caricatures – and do so to this day.

Ramon Allones Gigantes

Edward G. Robinson.

IN PRE-SECOND WORLD WAR Hollywood gangster
films, large cigars both represented power (as
frequently personified by Edward G. Robinson, himself
a keen cigar smoker) and mirrored the real-life
popularity of cigars with Mob bosses such as Al Capone.
Modern gangster films set in the pre-war era – such as
Brian De Palma's *The Untouchables* (1987), and his re-
make of *Scarface* (1983) – naturally also feature cigar
smoking. Wealth was also indicated by cigars in
melodramas of the period. In westerns, big cigars often
symbolized somebody crooked – such as the
unscrupulous railroad boss, the ruthless breaker of
Indian treaties, and the card shark. Small or thin cigars,
on the other hand, tended to suggest toughness or
meanness (think of Clint Eastwood in *The Good, the
Bad and the Ugly*: directed by cigar lover Sergio Leone).
On the rare occasions when women have smoked cigars
in Hollywood films, they have tended to suggest
mannishness or defiance. In the case of the period
comedy *Victor/Victoria* (1982), in which Julie Andrews
pretends to be a man, she smokes cigars to emphasize
her 'maleness'.

In French films, cigars have more usually been used to indicate style, elegance and good living. They have also symbolized joie de vivre and a free-wheeling attitude to life: Jean-Paul Belmondo in the gangster comedy *Borsalino* (1970) and the caper movie *That Man from Rio* (1964) spring to mind. Over the years, cigars have appeared relatively infrequently in British films dealing with contemporary subjects (although cigarettes were a regular feature), but when they appeared, particularly in dramas and comedies of the 1950s and early 1960s, they were often associated with cads and spivs. In a number of working-class-boy-made-good films of the 1960s, they often suggested that the hero felt he had 'arrived'. In British period films such as Joseph Losey's *The Go-Between* (1971), cigars have frequently been used to help recreate the past, upper and upper-middle class life in particular, without being used to any obvious symbolic effect other than indicating a male or leisured milieu.

Cigars in Hollywood comedies have also been used symbolically, either to indicate wealth or, in the case of Charlie Chaplin's films such as *City Lights* and *The Gold Rush* – where the little tramp smokes rich men's discarded cigar ends – poverty or the memory of it. But cigars have also provided invaluable props for comedians such as Harold Lloyd, Laurel and Hardy, W.C. Fields and George Burns, often used for visual gags. But the comedian with whom cigars are most readily associated, Groucho Marx (a cigar lover in real life), used his massive trademark stogie to give him something to do with his hands, and to emphasize the ludicrousness of the characters he played on the big screen. But he rarely, if ever, actually smoked it.

The public, not to say stereotypical, image of Hollywood movie producers and directors is of men with fat cigars in their mouths. And it is not without foundation. Producers and studio bosses such as Jack Warner and Darryl F. Zanuck (who actually owned a Cuban tobacco plantation) were dedicated cigar smokers. And directors such as Ernst Lubitsch, Orson Welles, Alfred Hitchcock and, more recently, Roman Polanski and Francis Ford Coppola have been equally keen, as was the British director of *Death Wish*, Michael Winner, until he stopped smoking a few years ago. Directors' love of cigars occasionally surfaces in their films: Welles, for instance, played the unscrupulous, cigar-chomping cop, Hank Quinlan in *Touch of Evil*, which he also directed; and Hitchcock's 1966 Cold War thriller *Torn Curtain* contains a scene in which an East German security man offers Paul Newman a cigar with the line: "Cuban – your loss, our gain." Although cigars are normally associated with power, in his 1946 film *Notorious*, Hitchcock depicted a wealthy Nazi sympathizer (played by Claude Rains) not only smoking cigars, but also referring to a

Opposite, *Groucho Marx.*

shipment of Havanas he is expecting. The character is weak, dominated by his mother and his love of cigars suggests a soft, pampered existence – in contrast to the tough, cigarette-smoking American secret agent played by Cary Grant.

On the whole, however, spy movies have pictured cigar smoking less than one might expect (is it that cigarettes impart a greater feeling of tension?), though cigars are featured in the 19th James Bond film, *The World is Not Enough*. In it, Cigar Girl, the Italian actress Grazia Cucinotta, hands over a box of cigars to an oil baron shortly before MI6 headquarters in London are blown up and she is seen making a high-speed getaway along the Thames. The script originally had her rolling a cigar on her thigh before the British intelligence building goes up in smoke. It's certainly a new twist on the old exploding cigar joke.

There are good reasons why so many directors like smoking cigars. The director's role includes making endless decisions in an often frenetic atmosphere and cigars offer the opportunity to think a little

Orson Welles.

longer the next time a question comes up, as well as helping the director to keep calm. They also convey a necessary sense of authority and serenity to everyone else on the set and help to pass the time between camera set-ups.

Paul Newman is one of many leading actors (others include Tom Cruise, Robert De Niro, Pierce Brosnan, actor/director Danny DeVito, Arnold Schwarzenegger, and Michael Caine) who are serious cigar smokers. Sometimes cigar-loving actors even get to smoke on screen. Jack Nicholson did as Colonel Jessep in *A Few Good Men* (directed by Rob Reiner in 1992), and earlier as the petty officer in *The Last Detail* (1973); Albert Finney played a tough cigar-smoking Irish political boss in the Coen brothers' period gangster picture *Miller's Crossing* (1990), and also smoked as the detective Hercule Poirot in *Murder on the Orient Express*; Michael Douglas smoked cigars as the odious "Greed is Good" character Gordon Gekko in the 1987 film *Wall Street* (films of the late 1980s and early 1990s portraying hard-nosed Yuppies often featured cigars); and James Woods did so as the semi-psychotic Max in Sergio Leone's 1984 gangster masterpiece *Once Upon A Time in America*. Arnold Schwarzennegger wielded a cigar in *Raw Deal*, Roger Moore in the James Bond Film *Live and Let Die*, and Robert Duvall in *Godfather II*. Cigar lover Sylvester Stallone got to smoke a cigar in Norman Jewison's 1978 trade union film *F.I.S.T*, but Sly's smoking scenes eventually hit the cutting room floor.

I should add that very few of these actors will actually have enjoyed the cigars they smoked on celluloid. The main reason is simple: continuity. Most directors will, if they can, avoid smoking scenes because of the difficulty of matching cigar lengths in different takes (cigarettes are easier). They will only use cigars if they are crucial to establishing a character or mood – and even then, they would prefer to film a cigar being lit or put out rather than actually being smoked. Eating scenes are, incidentally, an even bigger continuity nightmare. Nor do the props departments on feature films see it as their responsibility to store cigars perfectly – and hot studio lights don't help either.

The ultimate cigar film has to be *Smoke* (1995), directed by Wayne Wang from novelist Paul Auster's original screenplay. In it, the Brooklyn cigar store managed by Auggie Wren (played by Harvey Keitel, a cigar fan in real life) is the starting point for a number of tales including one in which $5,000 worth of illegally imported Cuban cigars manage to get accidentally destroyed. Wang and Auster shot a second film, *Blue in the Face*, set in the same store, immediately after filming *Smoke* – though, this time with special appearances from Madonna, Roseanne, Michael J. Fox and Lou Reed, as well as some of the cast of the original film, including Harvey Keitel.

THE CIGAR FROM LEAF TO PUFF OF SMOKE

HOW CIGARS
ARE MADE

*Above all, remember that
a cigar is an organic
product – despite the fact
that the journey from raw
leaf to finished cigar is a
complicated one, and that
each stage has to be
carefully controlled.*

AT THE PLANTATION

HANDMADE CIGARS are made of three constituent parts – the filler,
binder and the wrapper. Each of these parts has a different
function in cigar manufacture, and each makes a contribution to the
flavour and quality of a cigar. Tobacco leaves are grown and selected
according to which part of the cigar they are eventually destined.

The leaves also have to be cured to help preserve them, make them
suitably flexible, and to remove impurities. And they must be
fermented and matured – a further purification process which helps to
develop the required flavour – before they are finally rolled. The
process is not unlike wine making, where the quality of the grapes,
their growing conditions and the care taken over fermentation,
ageing and bottling are crucial to success. Unlike wine, however, the
production of top quality cigars is carried out almost entirely by hand.

The descriptions given here, and the technical terms used (unless
otherwise stated), are specific to Havana cigars, but the methods used
elsewhere are mostly similar.

Tobacco seeds are planted in level fields, so that they can't be washed away. Once they are planted, the seeds are usually protected from the sun and wind by a thin cloth or straw covering which is removed as they start germinating. The soil of the seedbed has to be well drained, and pesticides are used to protect the vulnerable seedlings from parasites.

After about five weeks (the second half of October in Cuba) the seedlings should be healthy and well-developed enough to be transplanted by hand to tobacco-growing fields, where they are carefully irrigated from below to help them survive. 200 square yards of seedbed (167 square metres) can produce anything between 15,000 to 25,000 plants, which are spaced around 2 feet apart, in rows which are themselves around 3 feet apart.

Right, *El Corojo wrapper plantation. The best cigar wrapper leaves are grown on sandy and sandy-loam soil, with filler and binder leaves best grown on silt-loam and clay-loam soils.*

The main growing season in the Pinar del Río area of Cuba, where the finest cigar tobacco comes from, is between November and February and takes place during *La Seca* (the dry season). By then, heavy rain during the previous months has ensured that the red soil is well irrigated. Growing conditions are ideal, with around eight hours a day of sunshine – the temperature hitting average highs of about 80F – and average humidity of 64 per cent. A high moisture content in both the soil and air is particularly important in the production of the thin, elastic leaf needed for the finest wrapper leaf – though over-watering, or too much rain is detrimental to leaf quality. Leaf production from transplantation to the end of the harvest takes around 120 days.

Left, *as the leaves grow, flower buds appear, and have to be removed by hand to prevent stunting of growth and deterioration of leaf quality (if the flowers were left alone, they would derive nutrients for growth from the leaves.*

Right, *cigar tobacco plants can produce between 16 and 20 leaves each, though their position on the stem will determine the precise use to which they will be put. The tobacco plant is normally divided into three parts: the top (corona), the middle and the bottom.*

Left, plants, of a type named corojo, cultivated specifically to provide wrapper leaves (essential for the finest cigars) are grown using a technique called tapado: the term means 'covering', in this case under muslin sheets held up by high wooden poles. The covering helps to prevent the leaves becoming too oily or coarse – as they would do in direct sunlight. The sheets are put in place, and removed, in due course, by men on stilts.

American Connecticut Shade wrapper leaves are produced in 10-foot-high cheesecloth tents in which the plants are similarly protected from the sun, and growing conditions are carefully controlled. A healthy wrapper plant can wrap up to 32 cigars. Growth of wrapper tobacco takes up to 90 days, depending on the weather; sun-grown filler and binder tobacco takes 45 to 70 days.

Leaves grown under direct sunlight – from the plant called criollo de sol – are classified by colour and texture into volado (literally: 'flown away'), seco (dry), ligero (light) and medio tiempo (half or average texture). There are similar classifications for wrapper leaves: viso (glossy), seco, amarillo (yellow), medio tiempo and quebrado (broken).

Right, sorting leaves. The ligero leaves from the top of the plant have a very strong flavour, seco leaves from the middle are much lighter and slow burning, whilst volado leaves add bulk to cigars and are used for their excellent burning qualities – from which their name presumably derives. The leaves are sorted by size and by physical condition (unhealthy or broken leaves end up in cigarettes or machine-made cigars).

When they are harvested, leaves – which are allowed to wilt slightly to reduce the danger of breakage – are removed singly using one hand movement. Those from wrapper plants are arranged in bundles. Wrapper leaves are removed in six phases – each taking around a week – starting from the base. These are called *libra de pie* (at the base), *uno y medio* (one-and-a-half), *centro ligero* (light centre), *centro fino* (thin centre), *centro gordo* (thick centre) and corona. The finest leaves are found in the middle of the plant. The uppermost leaves (corona) are usually too oily to be used for wrappers, except for domestic consumption, and are normally used as filler leaves. *Libra de pie* leaves are also rejected as wrappers.

After being sorted, the leaves are taken to a tobacco barn on the *vega* (plantation) to be cured. The barns have large doors at each end, and face west so that the sun heats one end in the morning, and the other in the late afternoon.

IN THE BARN

In the barn, needle and thread are used to string up the leaves in pairs on poles (*cujes*). The poles – carrying a hundred leaves each – are raised horizontally to a position high in the barn to allow air to circulate around them. Here the leaves are left to wilt, change colour and dry for between 45 and 60 days, depending on the weather. Temperature and humidity are carefully controlled, often by opening and closing the barn doors to adjust to changing conditions.

The next stage is the fermentation process, the main aim of which

Opposite, *leaves arrive at the curing barn.*

During the drying process, **right,** *the leaves turn to their characteristic brown colour, as green cholorophyll gives way to brown carotene, and the leaves oxidize. This method of air curing contrasts with the much shorter heat (or flue) curing methods used for cigarette tobacco. Once curing is complete, the different types of leaves are sorted into stacked bundles.*

is to remove impurities including nitrogen compounds, which produce the smell of ammonia. The nicotine content of the leaves can also be as much as halved during fermentation, and the level of acidity and tar is also reduced. Fermentation also helps the various types of leaves to attain a uniform colour and texture. The process is rather like composting, and is helped by the residual moisture in the leaves, which are placed in piles around 3 feet high and covered with jute.

Fermentation produces heat, but conditions are controlled so that none of the piles becomes hotter than 92F (33C). Once this first fermentation is complete – after around 35 to 40 days – the jute is removed, and the piles are broken up to enable the leaves to cool.

Now the leaves must be graded in the sorting house (*escogida*). The leaves are first shaken to separate them, and are then dampened with water and aired. The leaves are graded for different use (wrapper, filler or binder) and into as many as fifty different types according to colour, size and quality. Next comes the stripping process, during which filler leaves have part of their mid-ribs removed, and are flattened. The all-important wrapper leaves are stripped later, in the cigar factories themselves. The task of stripping is traditionally performed by women, often on a wooden board resting on their legs, giving rise to the fanciful myth of cigars being rolled on the thighs of Cuban maidens.

Left, *a fermenting stack. After grading, (see above) the leaves are flattened on boards, tied in bunches of 50, and sprayed with water (wrapper leaves) or a mixture of water and tobacco juice (filler and binder) and fermented again in large piles (burros) covered with hessian – which can be as much as 6 feet high – for between one and three months, depending on the destiny of the leaves involved. This second fermentation is much more powerful than the first. Normally ligero leaves are fermented for around 60 days, seco and volado for 40, and wrapper leaves (at a lower temperature) for 35 to 40 days. Thermometers are inserted into the fermenting leaves, and if the temperature reaches 110-112F (42-43C), the pile is 'turned': the leaves re-stacked to cool them, and to ensure that fermentation takes place evenly. They must also be classified once more before they can actually be used to make cigars.*

After the lengthy period of curing, grading and fermentation, the tobacco is finally ready to be sent to warehouses or factories in square bales (*tercios*). The palm bark they are wrapped in helps the leaves to stay at a constant humidity, and slowly to mature further until they are required for manufacture quite possibly as much as two years later.

*Top, checking fermentation. **Above,** unwrapping tercios before primary fermentation.*

In the case of some of the top Cuban brands, such as Cohiba, the ligero and seco leaves are selected once more, and fermented a third time in barrels in the cigar factory to ensure the finest flavour.

IN THE FACTORY

The production of a handmade Havana cigar involves more than 200 different stages, from seedbed to sale. The cigar factory is the place where all the effort put into growing and maturing finally comes together to produce the cigars we buy. This is where the skill of the rollers and a dedication to quality control on the part of the factory management will make or break a brand.

The wrapper leaves which arrive at the factory in bales (*tercios*) have to be taken out and shaken loose from each other. The *zafadores*, who perform this task, also have to dampen them (the operation is called *moja*), as by now they are fairly brittle as a result of losing moisture. To this end, the tips of the leaves are dipped in water, and the leaves are then sprayed. Excess water is removed by a further shaking. Finally, the leaves are hung in bunches for around 24 hours, with humidity kept at 95 per cent. The process gives the leaves a silky texture, with the finest of them almost translucent by the end.

Next, the wrapper leaves have their stems removed (the stems of the filler and binder leaves having been removed earlier – as outlined above).

The leaves are then graded once more by size and colour, stretched and flattened. Wrapper leaves are graded according to as many as 20 different classes. They are later gathered in bunches of 25, according to the size (*vitola*) of cigar for which they are destined. Each wrapper leaf should be enough for two cigars.

Filler and binder leaves have, meanwhile, been suitably combined, under conditions of great security in the blending room, though the ultimate blend in Cuba is up to the roller.

The following day, the blended leaves – in quantities sufficient to make 50 cigars – go to each roller.

Opposite, the Partagas factory; **left,** blender at work.

ROLLING CIGARS / 1

Rollers (torcedores), **right,**
work in large rooms, sitting at
benches which resemble
Victorian school desks. They are
pictures of intense concentration
combined with enthusiasm and
good humour. As they work,
they listen to extracts from
books and newspapers read
aloud by selected colleagues,
known as lectores. The
tradition dates from 1864,
when one of the most popular
books was The Count of
Monte Cristo, *published some*
20 years earlier. These days,
radio broadcasts are also part of
this effort to inform and educate
the rollers – as determined by
the Cuban government, at least;
and music is also played.
The torcedores *work up to 48*
hours a week and are paid
according to the number of
cigars they produce, typically a
few hundred dollars a month.
They can smoke as many cigars
as they like when they work,
and can take up to five cigars
home each day.

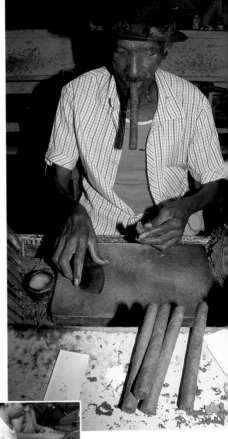

Left, *until the Cuban*
revolution, cigar rollers were
exclusively male, but now
women play an equal part in
this essential function.
Indeed, in the El Laguito
factory, famous for its
production of Cohibas, all
the rollers are female. There
are, typically, 200 to 300
rollers in a Havana factory.

Right, to make a handmade cigar, first two to four filler leaves (the number depends on the cigar's strength and size) have to be laid end to end and rolled into two half binder leaves. This is called the 'bunch'. The filler leaves, concertina'd along the length of the bunch, have to be carefully gathered and evenly

spread to make sure that the cigar draws properly. In the past, filler tobacco was sometimes arranged using a method (entubar) using up to eight narrow tubes of tobacco leaf rolled into the binder. Cigars made by this system tended to be very slow burning, but also ran the risk of the filler leaf becoming twisted, making the draw of smoke more difficult.

In the Philippines, they use a rolling method in which leaves are spiralled around two thin wooden sticks, which are removed after the cigar is wrapped.

Left, the filler blend, rolled into the binder, is then pressed into wooden moulds, a system in use since 1958.

ROLLING CIGARS / 2

Left, a mechanical press is then used to ensure consistency of shape. In Cuban factories, the buncher is also the roller – and sees the cigar through to the end. In other countries, such as the Dominican Republic, the tasks of bunching and rolling are performed by different specialists. In both cases, the roller starts his or her work with a supply of cylinders of moulded filler and binder tobacco appropriate to the size or brand being made. Most Cuban cigar factories make more than one brand, although they may specialize in a particular one. Around 60 sizes, some of them varying only slightly from one another, are available today.

Next, surplus filler has to be trimmed from the end of the bunch to leave a round top. The remaining stalk is now stripped from the binder, and a wrapper leaf is then selected. The wrapper is placed upside down and trimmed to the appropriate size using an oval steel blade called a chaveta, **left,** and **right.**

Left, the roller now positions the bunch (filler and binder) at an angle across the wrapper, which is then stretched and carefully wound around the bunch, using overlapping turns. After the final turn of the leaf, the wrapper is finally stuck down using a tiny drop of tragacanth vegetable gum, which is both flavourless and colourless. The roller then gently presses and rotates the cigar under the flat part of the chaveta to make sure that it is as even as possible. Apart from being essential to cigar making, the rollers' chavetas in Cuba are also used ceremonially: banged in unison on their desks as a greeting to visitors to the cigar factory.

Right, the final stage in making a handmade cigar is the cap. This is produced by cutting out a round piece of wrapper (about the size of a small coin) from the leaf trimmings. It is then stuck in position using gum. Occasionally, other ways of capping a cigar are used, normally for the finest cigars, and performed by the most skilled rollers. The 'flag' method uses the end of the wrapper leaf itself, smoothed down. In a variation (used with the Montecristo Especial, for instance), the 'mouth' end, or head, of the cigar is closed by twisting the end of the wrapper leaf. After the cap is made, the open end is guillotined to the correct length.

A skilled roller can make around 100 medium-sized cigars during an eight-hour day, with the fastest able to produce around 150. That's an average of no more than five minutes per cigar. The very largest sizes are produced much more slowly, at about half this rate, although one famous roller was able to make a prodigious 200 Montecristo As in a day: three to four times as many as his colleagues.

Each roller now uses a coloured ribbon – to identify the maker – to tie his or her cigars into bundles of 50. These are called *media ruedas*, or half wheels. The great majority of these bundles of finished cigars go directly to be treated against pests in a vacuum fumigation chamber. But, just as important, a number of bundles made by each roller are removed to be put through quality checks.

The percentage of cigars undergoing quality checks varies from factory to factory (and, therefore, from brand to brand). In the case of the most prestigious brands such as Cohiba, up to 20 per cent of the output might be checked. For other brands, only 10 per cent of cigars are typically examined. The tests are rigorous and detailed, checking aspects such as the smoothness of the wrapper, weight, length, firmness and general appearance – such as whether the ends have been cleanly guillotined.

Quality control in the large, state-of-the-art, mostly American-owned factories of the Dominican Republic is normally carried out using machines which, for instance, check suction, and, therefore, how well a cigar will draw. Machines are also used to check cigars at the bunch stage. But smaller manufacturers still prefer to do everything by hand.

In Cuba, quality control is also done by mouth. A number of cigars in the Havana factory are actually smoked by specialist testers. In these blind tastings, the professional smokers, or *catadores*, themselves tested a couple of times a year, have to report back on such criteria as draw, burning qualities and aroma for each brand and size. They work in the morning, smoking around an inch of each cigar, in between freshening their palates with plain tea. This way, the work of all the rollers in the factory gets checked.

Right, *quality controller.*

Left, *cigars in an* escaparate *(cooled cabinet).*

Cigars are removed from the fumigation chamber, and left in cooled cabinets, or *escaparates*, each holding up to 18,000 cigars, for three weeks or so. The idea is to slow down any further fermentation and remove any excess moisture.

Next, the cigars are graded. After being cooled, batches of a thousand of each type of brand and size are sorted by colour. There are around a dozen basic colour classifications, and more than 60 different shade categories – all of which the graders must be able to recognize. All the cigars of a given basic colour are packed into boxes, with the darkest positioned on the left, the lightest shade on the right, and intermediate shades in the middle.

Once the cigars have been colour graded, their brand bands are added, and they are put in the cedar boxes in which the consumer buys them. In the packing department, the cigars are checked once again for appearance, and those which have somehow evaded quality control are rejected. When they are placed in their boxes, the darkest cigars are again on the right, and the lightest on the left – though the colour of the cigars in each box should be pretty consistent. After they are checked again, a thin shaving of cedar is put on top of them, labels added to the box, and the box is sealed.

The boxes are then stored in carefully controlled conditions before being distributed for sale locally, or for export.

WHAT MAKES A GOOD CIGAR?

Avo XO Maestoso

– And why are the best cigars so expensive? Virtually every stage of tobacco growing and cigar manufacture contributes to the quality of a premium cigar – and to its price.

1 GROWING CONDITIONS

THESE ARE ESSENTIAL, especially for wrapper leaf (the *capa*), which needs virtually ideal conditions and is the most expensive part of a cigar. Good wrapper leaves come from very few sources, the finest of which is the Vuelta Abajo area of Cuba, but good non-Cuban wrappers are grown in Cameroon, Connecticut, Ecuador, Sumatra, Honduras, Mexico, Nicaragua and Costa Rica. The Dominican Republic, despite its large cigar industry, does not generally have suitable growing conditions for good wrapper tobacco, but since the mid-1990s there have been attempts to produce high quality wrappers, most notably and successfully by the Fuente family.

Criojo wrapper leaf.

2 THE WRAPPER

The wrapper leaf is also crucial to the appearance of a cigar, and gives it a bouquet (before it is smoked) which varies from brand to brand. The leaves must be smooth, without any projecting veins, undamaged, pliable (for ease of rolling) and not too oily, otherwise the wrapper would burn too fast. Wrappers are normally matured for between 12 and 18 months, and sometimes for longer. So-called green cigars once popular in the United States have wrapper leaves which are picked early. As they are not matured, the wrappers have little flavour or aroma.

3 MONITORING GROWTH

Another important factor is the care with which the leaves are grown, and how much their growth is monitored. They must be harvested at precisely the right time. It's a labour-intensive process, and the fact that leaves are picked singly, by hand, is a major cost factor. Each plant – in Cuba, at least – has to be visited an average of 170 times within a period of four months. As a rule, the longer tobacco leaves are exposed to the sun, together with the strength of the sunlight itself, the oilier and higher in sugar content they will be. This means that the leaves at the very top of a tobacco plant are normally the strongest in flavour.

4 FERMENTATION AND MATURING

Careful curing is crucial to the flexibility of the leaf when it is rolled, and the lengthy fermentation and maturing process is essential in producing the required flavour of the cigar leaves and the removal of impurities. Because of the fermentation process, cigar tobacco is much lower in tar, nicotine and acidity than cigarette tobacco.

If you can smell a vague odour of ammonia coming from a cigar, you can be sure the leaves haven't been properly matured. As a rule, the longer leaves are fermented and matured, the finer the flavour. However, flavour also depends on the careful selection and grading of leaves, and the way they are ultimately blended.

5 THE BINDER LEAF

The capote, or binder leaf, holds the cigar together, and is usually made from two halves of *volado* leaf from the bottom of the plant. This coarse leaf is chosen because of its strength. The fact that it has little flavour also means that it won't interfere with the filler blend.

6 THE FILLER

This is the key to the ultimate flavour of a cigar. Cuban cigars usually employ three different types of leaf for the filler (though in the larger sizes of some cigars, Montecristo for instance, a fourth type is also used; and sometimes only a couple of leaves are used for small sizes).

Ligero tobacco from the top of the plant is always placed in the middle of the cigar. It burns slowly, and this position helps to ensure even burning of the cigar as a whole. *Ligero* leaves are dark and full-flavoured as a result of oils produced by exposure to sunlight, and are – in every sense – central to the flavour of full-bodied cigars. They are matured for at least two years.

The ligero tobacco is blended with *seco* leaves (matured for some 18 months), which are considerably lighter in colour and flavour; and with *volado* leaves (matured for only nine months), which contribute their excellent burning qualities.

Partagas Corona

Hoyo de Monterrey Corona

Left and **below left,** *the proportion of different leaves in the filler determines the flavour of each brand. Full-bodied cigars, such as Partagas, have more* ligero; *whilst milder cigars (Hoyo de Monterrey, for instance) have a greater percentage of* volado *and* seco *leaves.*

Bolivar Royal Corona

The very full flavour of Cuban Bolivars, **left,** *actually comes from a blend in which there is more seco than volado, rather than reflecting a particularly high proportion of* ligero.

Hoyo de Monterrey Margarita

Small or thin cigars, **left,** *might well have no ligero tobacco at all – depending on the brand.*

Brands obviously have to have a consistent and distinct flavour – which means that the blend must always be the same, from year to year. The harvest in any one year might not always allow this, so big stocks of matured leaf from earlier harvests have to be on hand to ensure consistency. This stockpiling, too, adds to the cost of the finest cigars.

Of the seven worker grades in a Cuban cigar factory, the top four are rollers:

GRADE 4
The least experienced rollers. They only make cigars up to and including the petit corona size.

GRADE 5
The corona size and above.

GRADES 6 AND 7
The latter grade being confined to a few star rollers. Difficult specialist sizes such as piramides.

The roller's skill is reflected in the eventual cost of a cigar, and is why smaller sizes are relatively cheaper than bigger or more unusual ones.

7 HAND-ROLLING
Finally, premium cigars are hand-rolled, and as with any manual process, there is room for error. Not all cigars, even from the same factory, are equally well made. A skilled roller will naturally make better cigars than a novice (and it is worth noting that the bigger, and usually more fully flavoured sizes of any given brand, are made by the most experienced rollers). Apprenticeship for rollers takes nine months – an indication of what a skilled task the roller performs.

An over-filled, or badly-constructed cigar will have a frustratingly poor draw and need frequent re-lighting, impairing its flavour. If it is under-filled, it will burn too fast, resulting in a cigar which is too hot, and a rough smoke. Cigars must also look good and be properly stored. So careful quality control in the cigar factory is essential to the integrity of a brand and the price it can command.

The qualities in each category looked for by the *catadores* – the professional smokers of the Havana factory – vary according to the type of cigar. In robustos, or other fat cigars, for instance, the flavour is paramount; but in thin sizes, such as the slim panatela, good draw counts for more. Strict standards are set for each type of cigar.

Painstaking quality control, with its inevitable wastage, adds to the cost of handmade cigars. But the very fact that the finest cigars are made by hand, with room for human error, is what – even though it adds to the cost – makes them so superior to machine-made cigars.

HANDMADE OR MACHINE-MADE?

The primary difference between even the best machine-made cigars and handmade cigars is in the use of the long filler in handmade cigars.

THE TECHNIQUE of using separate leaves – carefully arranged concertina-style along the whole length of a cigar – can only be satisfactorily carried out by hand. It ensures that there is a passage through which smoke can be smoothly drawn. A cigar whose construction doesn't allow a smooth draw is not only frustrating to smoke, but will have to be frequently relit, impairing flavour. If the smoke draws too easily, the cigar will burn too fast, overheat, and produce acrid smoke. The long filler method allows a happy medium to be achieved.

'PAGES OF A BOOK'
This style of arranging the filler is sometimes referred to as the 'book' method. Unfortunately, the only way to check whether or not the method is being used (unless, of course, you are smoking a brand which you know to be handmade) is to cut the cigar lengthwise with a razor: the filler leaves should then look like the pages of a book.

BEST MACHINE-MADES

It's true that some of the best machine-made brands, such as Bering, use long fillers, but though they can offer a satisfactory smoke, they still can't really achieve the quality of handmade cigars. In the early 1990s, the Cubans went one further, by launching what they call 'hand-finished' machine-made cigars, such as the Quintero brand. They are made with long filler – bunched by machine – have caps similar to handmades and good wrappers. But they still can't quite match up. Confusingly, the Cubans now also produce handmade Quinteros. If you're not familiar with a brand, don't be fooled by terms such as 'hand-finished'. If a cigar isn't totally handmade, it's not handmade.

TELL-TALE CAP

A pretty good way of telling the difference between handmades and all but the best machine-mades is to look at a cigar's cap. The caps on machine-mades tend to be noticeably pointed, rather than smoothly curved. The cheapest machine-mades often come with no caps at all. Cigars with caps made using the 'flag' method described on page 71 can only be handmades – and usually amongst the best, given the skill needed to produce a smooth cap in this way. Of course, this criterion is difficult to apply to cigars such as pyramides and belicosos with deliberately pointed ends.

Caps of Saint Luis Rey Serie 'A'.

Paul Garmirian Belicoso

COARSE WRAPPER

The quality of leaves normally used for machine-made cigars is also inferior to the leaves used for handmades. The wrapper gives the best clue: likely to be coarse, and sometimes featuring protruding veins. Cost apart, the wrapper leaves have, by and large, to be coarser to withstand the machine making process – in sharp contrast to their tender manipulation by rollers.

WRAPPING

Cellophane wrapping on Cuban cigars is a definite indicator that they are machine-made, but not with non-Cuban brands, many of which, including some of the best, such as Macanudo, are individually wrapped in cellophane.

CONFUSION

To add to the confusion, a number of Cuban brands (such as H. Upmann and Punch) have machine-made sizes as well as handmade ones; and some Cuban brands which have been discontinued as handmades – La Flor de Cano and Por Larranaga, for instance – are still available as machine-mades. A number of non-Havana brands such as Dunhill (Dunhill Mild) and Bances also have machine-made cigars in their ranges.

And some very small sizes bearing famous names – usually identifiable by the fact that they have no caps, and are normally sold in cardboard cartons, are also machine-made. The type of cigar called cazadore, available in some Cuban bands is, although handmade, manufactured using off-cuts of leaf – and so inferior to regular handmades.

In the manufacture of the more expensive machine-mades, operators feed the filler tobacco into the hopper of a cigar-making machine, and place two binder leaves on a plate where they are cut. The two leaves are then positioned, overlapping, on a moving belt which feeds them into a rolling machine. Here, measured quantities of filler are wrapped and cigars emerge to be capped and trimmed.

With mass-market, machine-made brands, manufacture is similar to that of cigarettes. The filler blend (usually shredded leaf or scraps), is fed into rod-making machines and covered by binder leaf which has been processed into a continuous sheet. This creates a tube of the appropriate length. The wrapper – often made of rolls of reconstituted leaf – is then added in a similar way to the binder, and the cigars trimmed.

When these processes are compared to the painstaking construction and testing of handmade cigars, added to the use of inferior leaf for machine-mades (even if it isn't shredded), it is easy to see why such a difference in quality – and price – exists between the two.

CIGAR SIZES

The number of basic cigar sizes, the variations on these, and the plethora of names they are given by different brands is an area ripe for potential confusion.

Right,
sizing ruler.
Left,
*checking
thickness.*

HAVANA CIGAR RING GAUGE GUIDE

THE THICKNESS of a cigar has historically been expressed in terms of its ring gauge in ¹/64th of an inch. Thus, if a cigar has a ring gauge of 47, it is ⁴⁷/64ths of an inch in girth. By the same token, if a cigar had a ring gauge of 64, it would be an inch in diameter. Lengths are also normally given in inches and fractions of inches. Some of these ring gauges are now increasingly also being expressed in millimetres, and lengths in centimetres. That is the simple bit.

Avo Pyramid

STANDARD SIZES

The standard sizes (if it is possible to say they still exist) are, in my opinion, panatela, robusto, corona, double corona, especial, Lonsdale and Churchill. But it's impossible to be prescriptive about this – and these sizes not only have many variations (such as petit corona, corona extra and long panatela), but are also sometimes applied rather freely, not to say misleadingly.

Some brands use names such as Churchill, Rothschild or corona grande for cigars which are not, in the eyes of purists, any such thing. The Macanudo 'Baron de Rothschild', for instance, is technically a Lonsdale. The names robusto and Rothschild, incidentally, refer to the same basic size (a stocky, and usually punchy, cigar, 5 inches long with a ring gauge of 50). It could be argued that the corona is the basic cigar 'unit' (length 5 $1/2$ inches, ring gauge 42): it's certainly the size that gives rise to the greatest number of variations.

SPECIALIST SIZES

There are also various classic 'specialist' sizes such as tapering pyramides (the Cubans spell it piramide), and belicosos (sometimes incorrectly called 'torpedos') and cigars closed and pointed at both ends – technically called figurados. And there are rare but interesting oddities such as the culebras, found in the Partagas range, for instance: these are essentially three panatelas twisted together. Sometimes the term figurado is used for any unusually shaped cigar. The plethora of new brands over the last few years, with their own names (or numbers) for different sizes, has also added to the confusion.

Paul
Garmirian
Corona

EXTREME SIZES

Ring gauges for handmade cigars run from 26 (though many machine-mades are thinner) through to monster cigars, such as the Casa Blanca Jeroboam, with a ring gauge of 66 (over an inch thick, in other words). And lengths can vary from under 4 inches to 10 inches (in the case of the Royal Jamaica Ten Downing Street size, and indeed the Casa Blanca Jeroboam, once again). There can, of course, be any combination of length and ring gauge within those limits – and there often is. But, as ever, limits are made to be exceeded, and before World War II, the firm of Henry Clay (then a Havana brand) made the Koh-i-Noor for an Indian Maharaja. It was the largest smokeable cigar ever, weighing in at 18 inches long, with a ring gauge of a more modest 47. Not surprisingly, it was called the Visible Immenso, and the size was later recreated for King Farouk of Egypt.

Even bigger cigars have been made – but really only as novelties, and not to be smoked. In the Davidoff shop in London, you can see a cigar with a ring gauge of 96, measuring 3 feet long, just as – at the Partagas factory in Havana – they proudly show off a cigar almost 50 inches long. At the other end of the scale, the Bolivar Delgado, the world's smallest retailed handmade cigar, was a mere $1^1/2$ inches long.

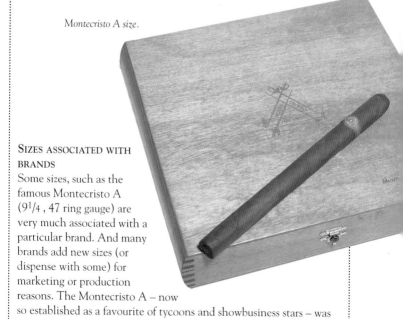

Montecristo A size.

SIZES ASSOCIATED WITH BRANDS

Some sizes, such as the famous Montecristo A ($9^1/4$, 47 ring gauge) are very much associated with a particular brand. And many brands add new sizes (or dispense with some) for marketing or production reasons. The Montecristo A – now so established as a favourite of tycoons and showbusiness stars – was only added to the Montecristo range in the early 1970s, as was the especial size.

In the same way, the Cohiba brand added five new sizes (the Siglo series) in 1992, and The Henry Clay brand (made in the Dominican Republic) added six new sizes in the late 1990s. The Havana brand, La Gloria Cubana, on the other hand, recently shed three sizes: though the non-Cuban brand bearing the same name added a few.

Cohiba's Siglo series.

Cohiba Siglo I   Cohiba Siglo II   Cohiba Siglo III   Cohiba Siglo IV

NUMBER OF SIZES PER BRAND

The number of sizes produced by each brand varies from a handful (four in the case of Cuaba) to literally dozens. The Partagas brand (Cuban version), for instance, comes in no fewer than 40 sizes – including machine-mades. The same applies to Romeo Y Julieta. Other brands such as Punch and Macanudo also have very big ranges – as the oldest brands have always tended to.

Most modern brands carry fewer than a dozen sizes. At the time of writing, the Trinidad brand, officially launched in 1998 only comes in one size, called fundador ($7^1/_2$ inches x 40), and even this one is different from the pre-launch version which, though it was the same length, had a ring gauge of 38.

There are over 40 Cuban handmade cigar sizes (and 69 sizes altogether if you add in machine-mades). In Cuba they all have factory names, most of which aren't normally used commercially for the Havanas we are familiar with. These include Mareva (petit corona), Prominente (double corona), Laguito No. 2 (Cohiba coronas especial), Laguito No. 3 (panatela), Julieta 2 (Churchill), Cervante, Londres and Dalia.

You will discover that different brands are better at producing some sizes than others, and that both flavour and quality of construction will often vary with size within a range. This is usually the case because many manufacturers like to offer a full range of sizes, even though some might be better advised to limit themselves to the ones they make best – either in terms of filler blend or the skill of their rollers. And only the greenest cigar novice would imagine that one brand's Churchill, say, is likely to taste like that of another: it almost certainly won't, and nor should it.

Cohiba Siglo V

BASIC HANDMADE SIZES

A number of basic handmade sizes, normally available, are listed below, but this table is only for guidance – for all the reasons given previously. Where appropriate, Cuban factory names are given in brackets.

NAME	LENGTH (INCHES)	RING GAUGE
Montecristo A (Gran Corona)	$9^1/4$	47
Double Corona (Prominente)	$7^5/8$	49
Especial (Laguito No. 1)	$7^1/2$	38
Long Panatela	7	36
Churchill (Julieta 2)	7	47
Lonsdale (Cervante)	$6^1/2$	42
Pyramide (Piramide)	$6^1/8$	52
Corona Extra (Corona Gorda)	$5^5/8$	46
Corona	$5^1/2$	42
Belicoso (Campana)	$5^1/2$	52
Robusto/Rothschild	5	50
Petit Corona (Mareva)	5	42
Panetela (Laguito No. 3)	$4^1/2$	26
Très Petit Corona (Perla)	4	40
Très Petit Corona	4	36
Demi-Tasse (Entreacto)	$3^7/8$	30

Hoyo de Monterrey Double Corona: 7⅝ inches (19 cm), ring gauge 49

Juan Clemente Especiales: 7½ inches (19 cm), ring gauge 38

Saint Luis Rey Churchill: 7 inches (17.5 cm), ring gauge 47

BASIC HANDMADE SIZES, CONTINUED

Casa Blanca Lonsdale: 6½ inches (16 cm), ring gauge 42

Hoyo de Monterrey Corona: 5½ inches (14 cm), ring gauge 42

Romeo Y Julieta Belicosos: 5½ inches (14 cm), ring gauge 52

Cohiba Robusto: 4⅞ inches (12.5 cm), ring gauge 50

Bolivar Petit Corona: 5½ inches (14 cm), ring gauge 42

Cohiba Panatela: 4½ inches (11 cm), ring gauge 26

CIGAR COLOURS

Cigar wrappers can come in more than 60 shades.
In Cuba these are given names such as encendido, colorado
encendido, sangre de toro, pajizo, clarisimo, colorado,
and colorado pajizo)*; but to simplify matters, shades can be*
reduced to seven basic colours.

Typical range of shades.

IT IS SOMETIMES THOUGHT that a dark wrapper necessarily indicates a
strong cigar, and a light wrapper a less full-bodied one. This is a
misconception, as the overall flavour of a cigar is determined by its
filler blend. Some manufacturers, however, choose light or dark
wrappers to indicate that their brand is either mild or full-flavoured.
The darker the colour, the richer and stronger the flavour of the
wrapper is likely to be, as it will have a higher oil and sugar content as
a result of having been on the plant for longer (and possibly from
nearer the top of it) and, therefore, exposed to more sunlight than a
lighter one. It might also have been fermented for longer: if so, it will
have lost more of its aroma than a pale wrapper might. But none of
this will be enough to have a significant influence on the overall taste
of a properly constructed cigar.

Sorting wrapper leaves by colour, size and texture.

The seven key cigar colours, in decreasing order of darkness, are:

Oscuro

Cigars of this colour are almost black (the same category is also sometimes called 'black' or 'negro'). *Oscuro* wrappers are from the top of the plant, where they have received more sun than the other leaves, and have also been fermented for longer. They have a very strong flavour, but hardly any bouquet. The popularity of this colour has waned, on the whole, but *oscuro* wrappers are still produced, mostly in Brazil, Mexico and Nicaragua.

Maduro

A very dark brown-black colour, similar to black coffee. The colour has recently become popular in the American market, and a number of brands now sport specifically *maduro* ranges. Sweetish *maduro* leaves – having had extra exposure to sunlight and greater fermentation – tend to be used to wrap full-bodied cigars. In Cuba they are the traditional wrapper for brands such as Partagas and Bolivar. They are often favoured by experienced smokers, rather than beginners.

Colorado maduro

These dark brown leaves have more aroma than *maduro* leaves and have a less strong, though rich, flavour. The colour is used for many cigars from Honduras.

A selection of pyramides.

COLORADO

A dark to medium, reddish-brown. *Colorado* wrappers have a noticeable aroma, and a rich flavour. It is the colour that you will recognize from well-matured cigars such as some of the classic Montecristo sizes.

COLORADO CLARO

Medium to light brown. Cameroon wrappers are often of this colour. The colour is also sometimes called 'natural', as occasionally is *claro*.

CLARO

A pale brown café au lait colour, often associated with Connecticut Shade wrappers and Cuban brands such as H. Upmann. The colour normally indicates a mild cigar.

DOUBLE CLARO

Greenish. Wrappers which are very mild, not to say bland in flavour, and low in oil content, making them somewhat brittle. The leaf is picked before it is fully matured, and then rapidly dried, sometimes using wood fires and even, in the past, using candles (hence the fact that this colour is sometimes called '*candela*'). The process allows the leaf to retain chlorophyll, and, therefore, its green colour.

The colour was once particularly popular in the United States and is also called American Market Selection (AMS) - as opposed to EMS (English Market Selection), which is used for the spectrum of brown wrappers. Double *claro* wrappers are used by American machine-made brands such as King Edward, and handmades such as Macanudo Jade.

THE CIGAR BOX

Cigar boxes are, for many cigar lovers,
one of the incidental pleasures of smoking.
The colourful images (called 'vistas'),
both inside and outside the box, with their historical references
and often gaudy border decorations, inspire a collectors'
passion in some smokers.

BOXING CIGARS, and labelling the boxes, is the last stage of production in the cigar factory. The boxes themselves – there are some 30 types altogether – are also normally made in the factory. Before it is packed, the box usually has paper, often coloured, sometimes waxed, gummed into it and used to cover the cigars. A seal is then added to the box before it finally awaits distribution.

Above and **right**, boxing cigars.

CEDAR

Spanish cedar, the wood used for cigar boxes and a member of the mahogany family, is perfect for cigar storage. It is slightly porous, and allows cigars to retain moisture and to continue to mature slowly – providing the box is properly stored. Cedar boxes stored in appropriately humidified conditions are excellent at absorbing the moisture in the surrounding air.

Before the introduction of cigar boxes, cigars were sold individually, or in bundles, often covered by palm leaves or pig's bladders. Later they were sold in large cedar chests capable of holding hundreds or thousands of cigars.

THE FIRST BOXES

The cigar box as we know it was first introduced in 1830, not by cigar makers, but by bankers. Though since the firm concerned was called Upmann, this might not be such a surprise. The bank was headquartered in London and its representatives in Cuba were in the habit of shipping back cigars for the use of the board of directors. For this, they chose cedar boxes, with the bank's logo stamped on them.

When, in 1844, Herman Upmann decided that the cigar trade was something to diversify into, the firm's cedar box was copied by other Cuban brands. By 1850, it had become the standard form of packaging. The use of boxes was also introduced in the United States after the Civil War, partly because this was required by internal revenue regulations so that officials could tax cigars accurately. Now the cedar box is used by almost all handmade brands. An unvarnished cedar box is also sometimes referred to as a *boîte nature*.

THE DECORATIONS

The lithographs adorning cigar boxes were the idea of Ramon Allones, an immigrant to Cuba from Galicia in Spain, who started the brand which bears his name in 1837. But by the mid-19th century, these colourful decorations took on an importance beyond mere embellishment. The burgeoning cigar industry meant that brands had to start differentiating themselves from their rivals: so box designs had to be as distinctive as possible.

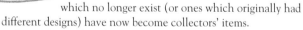

In the United States, things went further, with a plethora of eye-catching box designs, often garish or sentimental, being produced not only for the many brands themselves, but also for hotels, restaurants, bars and individuals. Among the most colourful of Havana box illustrations are those for Romeo Y Julieta, El Rey del Mundo, Saint Luis Rey and Ramon Allones. The H. Upmann vista shows a range of coins – not surprising given the brand's origins. The boxes and labels of brands which no longer exist (or ones which originally had different designs) have now become collectors' items.

Some Havana brands such as Cohiba and Montecristo use straightforward logos, as do non-Cuban brands including Ashton, Avo, C.A.O., Pleaides and Davidoff (which also did so when its cigars were produced in Cuba). This is becoming the trend among new or fairly modern brands – particularly those at the top of the premium cigar market.

Undecorated

Some cigar boxes, of the type called *corredeara*, are undecorated and merely embossed with the manufacturer's logo. Some cigars, such as many sizes of the Cohiba brand, are sold in varnished boxes. And boxes of a small number of cigars (usually five) are often made of cardboard (which is also the usual form of packaging for the majority of machine-made cigars).

Cohiba stamp.

Aluminium tubes, normally lined with a shaving of cedar, are also used for larger single cigars of both handmade and machine-made brands.

Some cigars, usually machine-made, come packed upright in glass jars. Cuban 'Country Cigars', which are sold in this way are, although hand-rolled, made with short filler, using leaf from the less good tobacco-growing areas of Cuba.

There is also a form of packaging called 8-9-8, used for some sizes of the Ramon Allones and Partagas ranges, for instance, and the Médaille D' Or part of the La Gloria Cubana brand. General Cigar actually produces a brand called the 8-9-8 Collection. The 8-9-8 box has curved edges and is polished. It contains 25 cigars, arranged in three layers with eight on top, nine in the middle, and eight on the bottom. The box adds to the cost of cigars sold in this way. Specially-designed packaging is also used for anniversary editions and to mark special occasions – such as the Millennium. And a variety of subtly different designs is often used to indicate the various lines within a brand: the dark green

Right, *pocket cigar cases for all occasions.*

Macanudo Robust box, for instance, as opposed to the mostly white box used for the bulk of the brand.

The increasing need for marketing and brand differentiation caused by the 1990s cigar boom has also led to manufacturers trying out new forms of packaging, such as the drum-style container used for Nat Sherman's Fifth Avenue selection.

SEALS, STAMPS AND CODES

After a box of any handmade type is filled, and the cigars in it have been checked for the last time, it is usually nailed tightly shut, and then sealed.

Warranty seal.

A label is normally used for this purpose. Most handmade brands follow the tradition of having a coloured seal, warranting authenticity. In the case of Cuban brands, individual brand seals were replaced, from 16th July 1912, by a standard green-and-white government label to guarantee that the cigars are genuine Havanas. The Havana seal reads: 'Cuban Government's warranty for cigars exported from Havana. *Republica de Cuba. Sello de garantía nacional de procedencia.*' The words in the first sentence are also translated (at the bottom of the label) into French and German.

The bottom of a handmade Cuban cigar box currently carries the words (in black): '*Hecho en Cuba. Totalmente a Mano*' – which translates as 'Made in Cuba. Completely by Hand'. They also carry a Habanos SA stamp, also in black, and a two- or three-letter factory code (in blue) and a four-letter date code. Since 1994, there has also been a printed chevron, with the word *Habanos* (in red) across one corner of the bottom of the box.

Cuban boxes also used to be stamped with the colour of the cigars in them, but this labelling hasn't been in use for some years: not least because it was often inaccurate.

There is normally a code on the bottom of the boxes of cigars made in the United States: a number identifying the manufacturer preceded by the letters TP. The code doesn't apply to imported cigars, even if made by American-owned companies.

Some brands refer to a 'vintage' on the box or aluminium tube. This is the year of the tobacco crop, not the year of manufacture.

THE CIGAR BAND

Adding the cigar band is the last task to be performed in the factory before the cigars have their final check and the box is closed and sealed. This is a skilled task: the band has to be closed with vegetable gum, with care taken that the gum doesn't get on to the cigar; and the bands have to be placed in exactly the same position on each cigar in a box, and on the same face of each cigar. If they aren't, the box may well not be what it says it is.

ORIGINS

THE ORIGIN of the band is shrouded in some mystery. One theory has it that bands were introduced because European smokers complained that their white evening gloves were becoming stained; another that they were initially used to ensure that badly-made cigars held together. Probably neither is true: certainly the latter is unlikely – no cigar should need a band to stop it from falling apart.

What is generally agreed, however, is that the band was first used by Gustave Bock, a Dutchman, and one of the first Europeans, other than those of Spanish origin, to get involved in the Havana cigar business. Whatever Bock's reasons for introducing the band (yet another suggestion is that German manufacturers were producing cigars which they passed off as Havanas), it is true to say that the use of bands was widespread by the 1850s. And by this time, the band had the same function as the decorated box: to differentiate, and to market, the many Havana brands. Bock's bands were printed in The Netherlands and, for a time, other manufacturers followed his example.

PERSONALIZED BANDS

As with cigar boxes and vistas, a proliferation of different, often personalized bands was soon available, particularly in the United States.
The Romeo Y Julieta brand was the first to introduce the concept of personalized bands in Cuba, a notion which appealed to wealthy smokers, such as the pianist Artur Rubinstein. Some famous smokers, such as Winston Churchill, even had sizes named after them; and others such as Bismarck and Edward VII (as well as U.S. Presidents for American brands) were depicted on bands.

In Cuba, at least, the custom of producing personalized bands stopped after the revolution. A collectors' market in bands now exists, but was at its strongest at the beginning of the 20th century. Prices now tend to be low for such a widespread and disposable item, except in the case of classic brands which have disappeared.

The bands of the longest-established brands are usually ornate, often using gold leaf, but more modern brands tend to keep it elegant and simple, frequently using plain logos.

A number of brands use more than one band design, or variations on a basic logo. Among Havanas, for instance, the Hoyo de Monterrey double corona, has a much fancier band than other cigars of the brand; and the Churchill size of Romeo Y Julieta has a plain, narrow gold band, whereas the other sizes all have red ones.

Dunhill Peravias

Dunhill Panatela

Nat Sherman Chelsea

Brands such as Nat Sherman and Dunhill have different coloured bands to designate different countries of origin or lines. In the case of Dunhill, the former Havana Dunhill band was red (and no longer in production), Dominican Dunhills have blue bands, and Canary Island Dunhill bands are brown.

Nat Sherman uses a clock logo, with different background colours to identify each line.

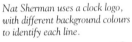

Cigars sold in so-called 'Cabinet Selection' form traditionally come without bands. They are usually packed in a deep cedar box containing 50 cigars, loosely arranged and tied together with silk ribbon. This 'half-wheel', as it is called, is the way cigars were usually packaged before the band was introduced. In Europe, some Honduras handmades are also often sold, usually singly, without bands, mostly for trademark reasons.

Oddly, it is still a matter of debate as to whether cigars should be smoked with the band on or off. In my opinion, it's completely up to you. As I've pointed out elsewhere, in Britain it was thought 'bad form' to show off the brand being smoked, particularly if it is a top premium cigar such as a Cohiba or Montecristo. This still applies to some extent, but that's a matter of etiquette which is increasingly ignored, and non-existent in the United States or Europe.

There is no reason why you should remove the band, but if you want to, wait until you have smoked the cigar for a minute or two. If you take off the band before you start smoking, you might risk damaging the wrapper – particularly if the band has been glued on tightly. But if you wait, the heat of the cigar will loosen the gum on the band, making it easier to take off.

SMOKING CIGARS

There's no great mystery to smoking a cigar correctly, and it's worth getting the basics right in order to ensure your enjoyment of an expensive product.

HANDMADE CIGARS need to be cut at the 'head', or closed end, before they can be smoked. There are a number of ways of doing this. You can use a sharp knife, you might use your fingernails, or you could – as the great majority of smokers do – use a cigar cutter.

Whatever you use, the key is to use something sharp, to make the cut quick, clean and level, and to leave the bottom of the cap intact – to avoid damaging the wrapper. There should be around $1/4$ to $1/8$ of an inch of cap left after you cut the cigar.

You can tell the very best cigars from the way they burn: they leave a much thinner carbon rim at the lit end than those of lower quality. A medium-sized cigar (such as a corona) should last around half an hour. Bigger cigars can easily take an hour or more to smoke. So choose a size appropriate to the amount of time you have at your disposal.

Any well-constructed handmade cigar should burn slowly and evenly – if it is properly lit. Well-matured, and older cigars (assuming they have been well stored) burn more smoothly than younger ones.

Figurados

These cigars (for example, the Havana Cuaba brand) are pointed at both ends and require their own lighting technique. The cap should be cut as normal, but the aperture at the foot of the cigar (which is small) doesn't need to be charred. Apply the flame and puff gently. The cigar should light very quickly as the tapered wrapper starts to burn. Once the cigar burns past the tapered section at the foot, it should burn much faster than a straight-sided cigar, or parejos. So it is essential to smoke a figurado slowly. Very popular in the 19th century, these are coming into their own again.

Cuaba Generosos

Warning

Some people like to warm the length of the cigar before lighting it. This is a custom which originated in the days of Sevillas, more than a century and a half ago. It is unnecessary today and indicates a lack of knowledge of cigars.

*Techniques demonstrated on **this page** and **opposite** by Edward Sahakian of Davidoff's London shop.*

Don't stick your cigar into port or brandy: this will spoil its delicate flavour, which is presumably why you have chosen to smoke it in the first place. Sip your drink separately. And never light someone else's cigar – as you might for a cigarette smoker. It's best done by the person who is smoking it, and he or she won't thank you if they take cigars seriously.

RELIGHTING A CIGAR

Don't worry if your cigar goes out – this sometimes happens, particularly when you are smoking the second half of the cigar. It also happens if the cigar is badly constructed and doesn't draw properly as a result.

Relighting

If it goes out, tap it gently to remove any ash. Now apply a flame to the perimeter of the end that was lit in order to burn away the edge of the wrapper. Blow through the cigar to get rid of any stale smoke in the filler. Then relight as you would a new cigar. A cigar will still offer a decent smoke if it has been left unlit for a couple of hours. Cigars with large ring gauges will be OK for even longer, particularly if you smoked less than half the cigar before it went out.

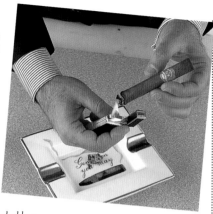

Don't constantly tap off the ash, while you smoke – as you would with a cigarette. You should let a cylinder of ash form (the more solid and regular it is, the better made the cigar). You will realize when it is ready to fall into the ashtray, normally when it's about an inch long, depending on the size and quality of the cigar. But don't be macho about it. There is no virtue in keeping a very long ash. It can impair draw, and you might find the ash falling off on to your clothes – which doesn't look cool.

Guillotine-type cutters are available in both single- or double-blade versions (my own preference is for the latter). They are small and portable, and range from very cheap plastic versions to staggeringly expensive pieces of jewellery. Your choice is a question of personal taste. All that really matters is that the cutter should be well balanced, easy to handle, and have a sharp blade.

Cigar scissors, often used in restaurants, are less portable than cigar cutters and take some getting used to. But if you use them properly, they are very effective.

If you find yourself without a cutter and want to use your fingernails, just pinch off the very top of the cap. Don't pierce it. This method of exposing the filler leaves compresses the tobacco and, therefore, interferes with the passage of smoke. It will make the cigar overheat. Some cutters work by taking a wedge out of the head of the cigar. They can also cause the same problem, and I suggest you avoid them.

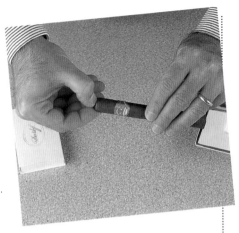

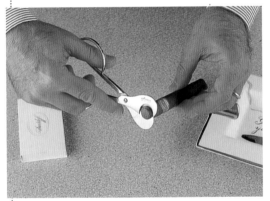

Cutting a cigar is one of the necessary rituals of smoking: do it with care. A badly-cut cigar will only hinder your enjoyment, and lead to frustration if you can't draw on it properly.

LIGHTING

The major consideration when lighting a premium cigar is an odourless flame. The second is to take your time.

Use a butane lighter rather than a gasoline one (unless you want the cigar to taste of petrol). Or use a normal wooden match – though allow it to burn a little before using it, to remove any sulphur. Avoid wax matches, or those with a high sulphur content: they too will impair the cigar's flavour.

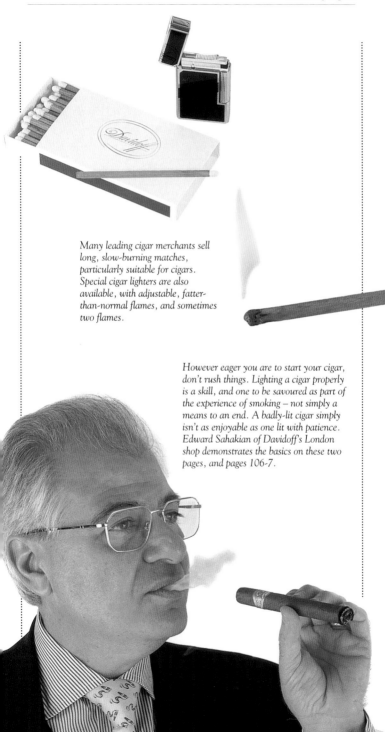

Many leading cigar merchants sell long, slow-burning matches, particularly suitable for cigars. Special cigar lighters are also available, with adjustable, fatter-than-normal flames, and sometimes two flames.

However eager you are to start your cigar, don't rush things. Lighting a cigar properly is a skill, and one to be savoured as part of the experience of smoking – not simply a means to an end. A badly-lit cigar simply isn't as enjoyable as one lit with patience. Edward Sahakian of Davidoff's London shop demonstrates the basics on these two pages, and pages 106-7.

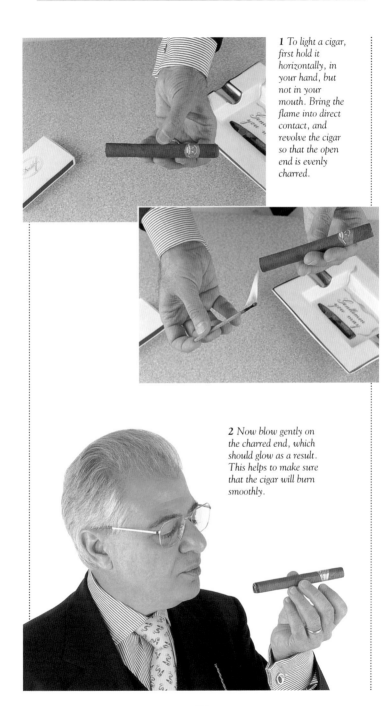

1 *To light a cigar, first hold it horizontally, in your hand, but not in your mouth. Bring the flame into direct contact, and revolve the cigar so that the open end is evenly charred.*

2 *Now blow gently on the charred end, which should glow as a result. This helps to make sure that the cigar will burn smoothly.*

3 At last you can put the cigar between your lips. Keep it as horizontal as possible. Hold the flame just away from the end of the cigar and draw air slowly through it whilst gently rotating the cigar with your fingers. It should ignite properly after ten or 15 seconds. To ensure that it burns evenly, you should now gently blow on the lit end again.

READY TO SMOKE

You should smoke slowly, without inhaling. If you inhale, the smoke, which is not only aromatic but alkaline, will make you cough. Instead, let the smoke circulate around your mouth. Don't drag on the cigar or puff it too often – unless you want to overheat it, spoiling the subtle flavour. Pause a little between puffs. Savour the cigar.

PUTTING OUT A CIGAR

If you start getting a noticeable aftertaste from a cigar, and the smoke becomes substantially hotter, (normally once you are within an inch or so of the middle of the band), it is time to give it up. But there is no need to stub it out, just lay it in the ashtray and it will quickly do the job by itself.

Get rid of the stub as soon as possible – to avoid the smell of stale smoke, which nobody finds attractive. Remember the words of the French actor Sacha Guitry: "If the birth of a genius resembles that of an idiot, the end of a Havana Corona resembles that of a five-cent cigar."

CHOOSING CIGARS

Bolivar Royal Corona

Saint Luis Rey Regios

Partagas Shorts

Some brands, such as Cuban Bolivars, Saint Luis Rey and Partagas are full-flavoured.

Selecting a cigar is a personal matter. It has to do with what is available to you, the size of your wallet and, above all, your own preferences in terms of size and flavour. There are no rules. What follow are thoughts which may help if you are new, or relatively new to cigars.

THERE IS NO such thing as the 'best' cigar – only cigars you like and ones you don't much care for. Don't be afraid of trying out different brands and sizes: it's the best way of learning about cigars – and the more you know what you don't like, the greater will be your appreciation of the cigars you like. If you want to compare cigars, don't forget to take into account the time of day, whether you have just had a meal and your mood. It's best to compare cigars in similar conditions.

The cigar department, Harrods, London.

Cohiba Exquisito

Cuaba Divinos

There are a number of factors you should take into account when choosing a cigar. These are brand (and country of origin), size, appearance, and bouquet (the smell of the cigar, particularly the wrapper) before you have smoked it; and flavour and quality of burning and draw while you are smoking. The draw (which tells you about the quality of the cigar's construction) should be easy, the smoke not too hot or acrid, and the cigar should not have to be constantly relit.

Dunhill Romanas

Excalibur No. IV

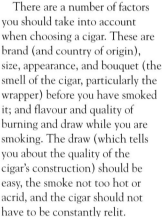

BRAND AND COUNTRY OF ORIGIN

It may seem obvious, but different brands have distinctive flavours (or should have) because of their individual filler blends. Leaves from different countries also tend to have their own qualities.

Montecristo No. 5

Paul Garmirian Corona

Some brands – including Cohiba, Cuaba, Dominican Dunhills, Excalibur, Montecristo and Paul Garmirian – can be classified as medium to full.

Arturo Fuente Petit Corona

Avo No. 2

Joya de Nicaragua Elegante

Davidoff Double R

Romeo Y Julieta Exhibición No. 4

Punch Double Corona

Some lines within large brands are deliberately blended to be either milder or fuller-bodied than the brand as a whole. A typical example is the Robust line of the otherwise mild Macanudo brand. Others, like Arturo Fuente, Avo, Joya de Nicaragua, Davidoff, and the Cuban Romeo Y Julieta and Punch brands are mild to medium in flavour.

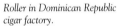

Roller in Dominican Republic cigar factory.

As for country of origin, it is worth noting that all Havana cigars are made from Cuban leaf, and (although there are some mild brands) are generally medium or full-bodied.

Cigars made in the Dominican Republic, Honduras, Jamaica and Mexico are normally made of leaves from more than one country. In the case of Honduran, Jamaican and Dominican cigars, the wrappers used are often Connecticut Shade leaf, but wrappers from Cameroon, Sumatra and other areas are also used. And many of the brands made in the United States, the Dominican Republic and Honduras use leaf grown from seed of Cuban origin – all adding to the difficulty of making sweeping generalizations about the flavour associated with cigars from a particular country.

Macanudo Duke of Devon

Pleiades Orion

Royal Jamaica Double Corona

Ashton No.40 Maduro

Rafael Gonzalez Très Petit Lonsdale

H.Upmann Pequenos No. 100

Cigars such as Macanudo, Pleiades, Royal Jamaica, Ashton, the Havana Rafael Gonzalez and the H.Upmann brands are normally mild.

SIZE

Cigars with larger ring gauges (corona and above) are usually made by the most experienced rollers, and contain more tobacco per inch, so they are likely to be better made than the small sizes of a particular brand and to offer a slower, smoother smoke. Because they are made by the best rollers, they are also relatively more expensive.

As a rule, cigars with large ring gauges tend to be the most full-flavoured of a particular line or brand – because there is usually less volado and more ligero leaf (see page 61) in the filler blend. But this is no guide when comparing different brands. Smaller sizes of a given brand often have little or no ligero leaf. But the largest sizes of a mild brand are likely to be milder than the smaller sizes of a full-bodied brand. Because of the better quality of construction, seasoned smokers – particularly those not pressed for time – often prefer to smoke the larger sizes of their chosen brand.

But what should the novice smoker start with? In my opinion, beginners should start with fairly small cigars of a mild brand – such as a petit corona (mareva) – and then progress to larger sizes such as corona and Lonsdale. But there is no reason why you shouldn't leap in at the deep end with a Churchill or robusto – though I do advise a mild or medium brand.

It's worth keeping a stock of cigars of varying sizes and strengths – as you may well want to smoke different cigars in different situations. Many smokers, for instance, prefer to start the day with small or mild cigars, reserving fuller-bodied cigars for the afternoon and evening – or after dinner. The robusto (Rothschild) size has, however, become very popular – particularly in the United States – for a short but punchy smoke after a heavy lunch. A large full-bodied cigar after dinner, or a big meal, makes sense. This is because it will last long enough for after-dinner conversation, and will be more pleasurable and satisfying to smoke on a full stomach than a small or mild cigar. Such a cigar (a double corona or Churchill, for instance) is less advisable before a meal. It will not only diminish your appetite, but will

Punch Petit Corona

reduce your appreciation of food and, more particularly, wine. A full-bodied cigar with port, whisky or brandy, however, can positively enhance your enjoyment of those drinks. But if you prefer a mild or small cigar after dinner, it's entirely up to you. However, it makes no sense to smoke a mild cigar after a strong one. Always move from mild to strong.

There is no such thing as the best size to smoke. There has been much written about this in cigar literature of the past, particularly by the great Zino Davidoff, who quotes the painter, Kees Van Dongen, as saying: "The cigar, like the pipe, ought to match your physique". And the Cubans have an old saying, "as you approach 30, you have a 30 ring gauge; as you approach 50, you have a 50 ring gauge." You can ignore this. But bear in mind that somebody very thin smoking a long, fat cigar can look silly, ostentatious or pompous.

APPEARANCE AND BOUQUET

The first thing to do when you choose a cigar is look at it. The wrapper should have a slight sheen. It should also be undamaged, without any noticeable veins. If it is at all damaged, reject it.

It should not be too brittle or dry (something you can only judge if you have smoked or handled well-stored cigars). Then, don't be afraid of feeling it gently: it shouldn't be soft to the touch, but nor should it be too stiff. This judgement, again, will only come with experience. An over-soft cigar will be poorly filled and burn too fast; a cigar which is too firm will draw badly. Then smell the cigar – it should have a pleasant aroma, subtle but noticeable. If it doesn't, except in the case of very dark cigars or greenish double *claro* cigars, it has probably been badly stored. If it has a vague hint of ammonia about it, it hasn't been properly fermented, or matured for long enough.

Don't, whatever you do, roll a cigar next to your ear. This custom is contemptuously known in the cigar trade, as 'listening to the band', and will mark you down as a complete novice. It will tell you nothing about the cigar, and can also damage it. I can't find an authority prepared to say how this habit arose, but perhaps it was to check for dryness.

A cigar's wrapper colour can give you some idea of its flavour – although remember that it is the filler blend rather than the wrapper that really counts. Manufacturers are increasingly labelling their cigars as mild, medium or full-bodied by their choice of wrapper colour. Dark wrappers (in themselves sweeter and oilier than lighter ones) normally indicate fuller-bodied cigars, and lighter ones (particularly Connecticut Shade) milder cigars. But it is perfectly possible to have a full-bodied cigar with a pale wrapper or a mild cigar with a very dark wrapper. Darker cigars are also often more matured than lighter ones: but this, too, is not an invariable guide.

CIGARS FOR WOMEN

What cigars should women smoke? The simple answer is: the same cigars as men. By which I mean, whatever they enjoy and feel comfortable with. If you are a woman reading this book, it could be that you are an inexperienced cigar smoker. In which case, start with a mild brand, and a smallish size (such as a panatela). Don't, however, start with the very smallest sizes, as you really won't get an impression of what serious cigar smoking is about. And you might also like to think of your appearance – a slimmer cigar will probably suit you best, and look more elegant.

After trying the smallest sizes, try moving up to sizes with ring gauges of 42 or perhaps less, such as especial, long panatela, Lonsdale and corona. You will find a full range of flavours in these sizes across the different brands.

WHAT TO DRINK WITH CIGARS

Matching a drink to a cigar is very much like matching food to wine. And whilst the first rule is that there are no rules, a little thought and experimentation will show that some combinations work better than others.

As with wine and food, the aim is to achieve balance and harmony, with neither the cigar nor the drink overpowering the other. In general, stronger, full-bodied drinks are preferable to lighter ones – although time and place will affect our overall enjoyment. After a long, hot summer's day, a cold beer and a small cigar can be perfect.

But on grander occasions, a grander cigar is called for, and a more careful match has to be made.

Cigars and brandy are a classic combination, so much so that for many years, Martell's advertisements all included a corpulent gentleman holding a brandy balloon in one hand and a cigar in the other. Nowadays, they find this faintly embarrassing, as neither the man's, nor the glass's shape is currently in fashion. But there's no doubt that cigars and brandy complement one another.

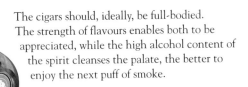

The cigars should, ideally, be full-bodied. The strength of flavours enables both to be appreciated, while the high alcohol content of the spirit cleanses the palate, the better to enjoy the next puff of smoke.

For expert advice on this topic, I have consulted Godfrey Spence, distinguished author of *The Port Companion*, and Senior Lecturer at the U.K.'s Wine and Spirit Education Trust. While happy to give advice for everyday drinkers and smokers, he reminds me that smoking is strictly forbidden at professional wine tastings. The merest whiff of cigar or cigarette smoke will impair the flavours and aromas of fine wines.

Very sweet spirits, such as Grand Marnier (and others shown here) don't go well with cigars; nor does the dryness of gin.So brandy, which is between these two extremes, usually makes the best match.

So perfect is this match between cigar and cognac that a number of cognac houses have blended spirits specially for cigar smokers. Jaques Hine devoted many years of painstaking, if enjoyable, research to find the ideal blend. The firm now sells Hine Cigar Reserve, initially aimed at the restaurant trade, but recently more generally available, at around £50 a bottle in Britain. It need hardly be said that for the finest cigars, only very good brandy will do. It needn't only be Cognac or Armagnac: the very best Spanish brandies are also in the running.

Mild cigars work very well with the delicate, smoky character of Highland malts and the better-blended whiskies. For stronger cigars, I recommend a pungent Islay whisky such as Lagavulin or Ardbeg.

It's also worth copying the foodie's trick of trying to match cigars with spirits from their country of origin – as foodies do with ingredients. Forget the frivolous rum cocktails, and the ubiquitous Bacardi: try fine golden rum, matured in wood, and a handmade cigar. Drink it straight, or on the rocks: potentially, a great combination.

No wine connoisseur would allow cigars, however good, to spoil the delicate flavours of champagne, fine claret or burgundy. However, the more robust fortified wines, such as port or sherry, can stand up to cigar smoke and work well with it. Full-bodied sherry can live with medium-bodied cigars; and lighter sherries with mild ones. Port and cigars have gone together since the 19th century. I know a wine expert whose personal preference is rich, aged tawny port, or an equivalent aged *colheita*, to drink with a cigar. Vintage port he finds more troublesome. The long ageing required brings finesse but, he warns, leads to fragility in some wines. At the time of writing, the 1983 vintage seems to be a good compromise: maturing nicely, the port still has the necessary concentration to meld with cigars.

BUYING CIGARS

Harrods' cigar department, London.

First, find a helpful cigar merchant. This is becoming easier now that cigars are fashionable again. Apart from specialist cigar shops, many department stores (such as Selfridges and Harrods in London, whose cigar shops are run by the highly respected firm of James J. Fox and Robert Lewis) also have good selections of well-kept cigars. And an increasing number of bars, and restaurants are taking cigars very seriously – quite apart from the many cigar bars which have sprung up around the world.

MAIL ORDER AND INTERNET

YOU CAN ALSO order cigars on the Internet from long-established firms such as Nat Sherman in New York or newer outfits such as Cigars Direct in Britain. There are also other, long-established, mail order cigar companies such as Lew Rothman's J.R. Tobacco – which, together with its retail and wholesale business, is involved in the sale of around 40 per cent of all premium cigars in the United States, often at bargain prices.

However, convenient as these methods may be, there is no substitute for actually seeing what you are buying. Remember, too, that, even if well packed, cigars can be damaged, or become dried out in transit, or if the box is opened by customs.

CHECKING CONDITION

How well a cigar has been stored is crucial to its condition and, therefore, likely to affect how well it smokes. You should always examine handmade cigars before buying them. If they are in a box, ask for it to be opened. Any respectable cigar merchant should allow this – and you should worry if he (or increasingly, she) doesn't.

The cigars should look as if they are in good condition. If you don't like the look of the cigars, don't buy them. All the bands in the box should be in the same position, and the turns on the wrapper leaves should spiral in the same direction. The cigars should be the same basic colour, with the lightest shades on the right and the darkest on the left. If this isn't the case, hesitate before buying the box. Any of these deficiencies could point to a lapse in quality control at the factory, the possibility that some of the cigars have come from another box (if it is already open), or that it has been previously opened (by customs, for instance).

Sniff one or two of the cigars to see if you like the bouquet. You might also take a cigar out of the box and smell the gap left by it – this is the best way of appreciating the bouquet, bearing in mind that older cigars, or those with very dark wrappers, are likely to have a less pronounced bouquet in the first place, however good they may be.

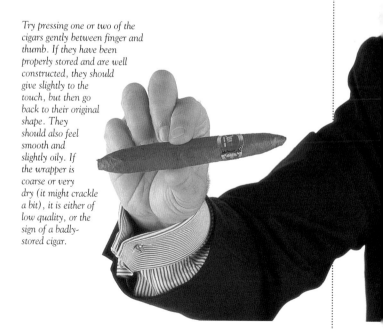

Try pressing one or two of the cigars gently between finger and thumb. If they have been properly stored and are well constructed, they should give slightly to the touch, but then go back to their original shape. They should also feel smooth and slightly oily. If the wrapper is coarse or very dry (it might crackle a bit), it is either of low quality, or the sign of a badly-stored cigar.

Of course, if you completely trust your cigar merchant, the precautions described here may not be necessary. But I think it's always worth checking what you buy, if only cursorily.

This is particularly true today, when there are so many fake cigars on the market, not least in the United States, which is plagued by the so-called Don Nobodies: badly-made and badly-matured cigars which undercut established brands in price. In the United States, there has also been a recent surge in the smuggling of contraband Havana cigars across the border with Mexico, often purchased in Tijuana. Many of these are probably counterfeit or cheaper brands masquerading as more expensive ones. In 1998, the U.S. Customs Service seized contraband cigars valued at around $1.6 million.

At the time of writing, Cuban cigars can't be officially sold in America thanks to the government embargo (only up to about $110 worth of Havanas can be brought into the country, for personal use). This means that the biggest sizes of top brands such as Montecristo and Cohiba can sell for over $100 each on the black market. Outside the United States, there is also the problem of trying to distinguish non-Cuban versions of famous brands from their Havana counterparts.

Check the green and white Havana seal: it has been the same since 1912, and the colours and text do not vary.

Then look at the bottom of the box. Check that the box carries the black stamp reading: Hecho en Cuba. Totalmente a Mano. This is what tells you that the cigars are completely handmade, though the box could, of course, be faked, or machine-mades substituted for the real thing. However, this legend, introduced in 1989, is a crucial safeguard.

HOW TO READ
A CIGAR BOX

With Havana brands, it is essential to 'read' the box, unless your cigar merchant has an established reputation. This is not only to try to eliminate fakes, but also to make sure that you aren't buying machine-made versions of famous Cuban brands, or non-Cuban brands using the same names and very similar logos or vistas as the Havana originals.

Pre-1989 Havana boxes of handmade cigars used to read Hecho a Mano *(without the word totalmente). These may well be OK, but if you want to play it safe, only go for boxes with the* Hecho en Cuba. Totalmente a Mano *legend.*

These days, Hecho a Mano only means hand-finished – not completely handmade, and Hecho en Cuba by itself can only mean machine-made. Boxes of pre-revolutionary handmades (not that you are very likely to come across them in normal circumstances) read 'Made in Havana, Cuba'.

Don't be fooled by non-Havana boxes which say, 'Hand-rolled'. This doesn't mean handmade, only that the wrapper has been added by hand to machine-made cigars. Envuelto a mano merely means hand-packed.

Check also for the black Habanos S.A. stamp and the printed chevron bearing the words 'Habanos' (red on white). There should also be a two- or three-letter factory mark, introduced in 1985. If the box doesn't carry the Habanos S.A. stamp, but does have a stamp reading Cubatabaco, it is possibly pre-1994. The Cubatabaco logo was applied to Havana boxes between 1985 and late 1994.

The vistas and decoration on the boxes of non-Havana cigars with Cuban brand names, as well as the bands, tend to be similar to the Havana originals, usually varying only in small details. On the bands of Dominican H. Upmanns, for instance, the year 1844 (the year of the brand's founding) is substituted for the word *Habana* found on the Cuban originals. I must stress that these non-Havana handmades bearing famous Cuban names are often excellent cigars in their own right (though normally bearing no similarity in flavour) – but it is in the manufacturers' interest to make you think you might be buying Havanas. In reputable shops in the United States, they couldn't possibly be Cuban cigars while the embargo continues, but elsewhere, you could be fooled if you don't carefully inspect what you are buying.

The term Havana (or Habanos), incidentally, is technically only applied to cigars wholly made by leaf from the Pinar del Río area of Cuba. Cigars made from tobacco from other parts of Cuba don't count as real Havanas.

Extra precautions to exclude fake Havanas have been taken in the British market with the introduction of labels (in a corner, on the bottom of the box) with the letters EMS (standing for English Market Selection) with the colours now changed every year as an extra security measure.

You can also date the cigars from the colour of the EMS label. Thus, for instance, green labels were used for boxes clearing British customs from 1992 to October 1997. Those imported from November 1997 and September 1998 were pink, those for the year following were pale blue; and yellow was chosen for 2000.

FACTORY MARKS

From 1985 until 1999, it was possible to work out not only which factory a box of Havana cigars had come from, but also the month and year of manufacture. But that is no longer possible. A two- or three-letter code in blue ink was used for the former, and a four-letter code (based on the word *NIVELACUSO*), representing the numbers one to ten, for the latter. The factory code, in particular, was an important source of information. Many brands of Havanas are made by more than one factory: and they are, to be frank, not equally well made from factory to factory. Some factories specialize in certain brands, though will make others if demand makes it necessary. It is worth noting that half of all the handmade cigars exported from Cuba in the 1980s were Montecristos – even though only three factories could have been said to specialize in them at the time. Many Montecristos, in other words – not made in those three factories – were not as good as they should have been.

The old factory code used initials based on post-revolutionary names for the factories of famous brands. There were, of course, also codes for newer factories. Thus, for instance, EL denoted El Laguito (home of the Cohiba); HM for Heroes del Moncada (formerly El Rey del Mundo); JM for José Martí (once the H. Upmann factory, and now also the source of some of the best Montecristos); FPG was the designation of what was once the Partagas factory – and still makes amongst the best Partagas, as well as good Montecristos; FR was the Fernando Roig factory (formerly La Corona); and BM stood for the Romeo Y Julieta factory, now called Briones Montoto. But my own writing, as well as that of others, revealed these codes, and led to many smokers checking their boxes. As a result, in January 1999, a new system was introduced to scramble both the factory and the date codes. The first new version of the date code was broken, and revealed on the Internet, within eight weeks of being introduced. Now (since August 1999) the factory codes are changed every month, and the date codes have also been changed once again, and haven't been broken at time of writing. But that shouldn't stop you from checking the pre-1999 boxes, of which there are still plenty around.

ALUMINIUM TUBES

If you want to buy a single cigar, some brands (including Romeo Y Julieta and Dunhill) are available in aluminium tubes lined with cedar, originally used by H. Upmann. The tube of the Romeo Y Julieta Churchill size states: 'The rich aromatic flavor of this fine Havana cigar will be protected by the aluminium container until opened.' But, even so, smoke it soon: the tubes aren't completely airtight – so the cigars may become slightly

Famous brands in aluminium tubes – but beware, they could be machine-mades: see page 124.

dry, and lose their bouquet; nor are they likely to be as well matured as cigars in boxes – though they can still be very satisfactory. And, remember, you have fewer clues as to their origins, particularly as many Havana machine-mades bearing famous brand names come in tubes.

WRAPPED IN CELLOPHANE
Havana cigars wrapped individually in cellophane are almost certainly machine-made, though the situation is complicated by the fact that a handful of brands, including some sizes of Cohiba, when sold in small packs, come wrapped in this way. Many excellent handmade cigars originating in countries other than Cuba are also packaged in cellophane. Cigars wrapped in cellophane keep well as there is less chance of them drying out than those left naked in cedar boxes, but they mature less.

CIGAR SHOPS
One of the undeniable pleasures of smoking handmade cigars is visiting one of the great cigar shops. Some of them fascinating in themselves; all of them are an experience for the senses, creating a keen anticipation of the smoking pleasure to come.

Cigar heaven, in terms of the greatest concentration of fine tobacco shops, is to be found in the St. James's area of London – just off Piccadilly.

Fox Epicures in a golden alligator leather travel humidor.

ROBERT LEWIS
London established itself as one of the great centres of the Havana cigar trade – if not the greatest – in the early 19th century. And the earliest established shop, founded in 1787, in Covent Garden, was Robert Lewis. It was actually founded by Welshman Christopher Lewis, but made prosperous by his relation, Robert. The firm sold the first Havanas to reach London in 1830. After a couple of moves in the early 19th century, the company opened a shop at 81 St. James's Street in 1834, in an area famous for its gentlemen's clubs.

It eventually moved to 19 St.

James's Street, where it still exists with its male and club-like aura, though now acquired by the once rival firm of James J. Fox. The merger took place in 1992. Fox's (as it was known) was originally founded in Dublin in 1881, with its original London shop opening in 1946.

The merged firm recently opened a cigar museum on the premises, at the back of the ground floor, although many of the items on display have been in the shop for many years. Exhibits include what are probably the oldest cigars in existence – a box dating from the Great Exhibition in 1851. You can also see Winston Churchill's account and many other fascinating treasures.

In 1997, the firm launched its own brand of full-bodied Dominican-made cigars. The firm also has a very good website, from which you can order cigars and accessories, though they warn American customers against trying to order Havana cigars. The Cuban author G. Cabrera Infante once wrote of the shop (in his book *Holy Smoke*): 'If I had to live in a shop I would dwell in Robert Lewis forever...'

DAVIDOFF

Round the corner, at the junction of Jermyn Street and St. James's, is the London Davidoff shop (35 St. James's Street). The shop, founded in 1980, presents, with its modern decoration, quite a contrast to James J. Fox and Robert Lewis. Here you can find Davidoffs, of course, but also everything else you might need as a smoker, from the most basic machine-made cigars to the finest handmades from around the world (as well as an impressive range of cigarettes) and accessories galore.

*Davidoff's St. James's shop, **above**, is the home of a cigar 3 feet long, with a ring gauge of 96 (that's 1^1/2 inches in diameter). The shop also has occasional displays of rolling, and British launches of new brands or lines sometimes take place there.*

The shop, under the aegis of the kindly and extremely knowledgeable Edward Sahakian (or his son, Eddie, brought up in the business) sells well over 400,000 cigars a year in a bewildering array of shapes and sizes – boxed and single – over half of them handmades.

Edward Sahakian in the Davidoff shop's Havana room.

The finest are displayed in the humidor room, in open boxes which you can examine. In the basement are kept not only more of the shop's stock of cigars, but also the stocks of its many famous customers.

ALFRED DUNHILL

Not far from the Davidoff shop is one with a very different character again, and one of the most famous names in the world of tobacco: Alfred Dunhill, at 30 Duke Street.

The shop, though bombed during the war and rebuilt, has been on the same corner site since 1907. These days, it sells clothes and accessories, as well as cigars.

The famous humidor room, which used to be rather hidden at the back of the store, is now more centrally placed on the mezzanine floor following a major renovation of the shop in 1997. Different Havana brands are housed in large cedar cabinets in this elegant and traditionally decorated room, and metal gates lead to private lockers (or keeps) containing the stocks of customers who have bought ten or more boxes of cigars and have left them for ageing. There are more than 50,000 cigars stored in the Keep, whose lockers are identified only by number. Alfred Dunhill himself pioneered the use of humidification in the 1920s, so it is only to be expected that the climate in the humidor room is perfect for cigar storage, and monitored by the very latest equipment.

SAUTTER

Some distance away is Sautter of Mayfair (106 Mount Street), a small shop with a convivial owner, Desmond Sautter. It is a happy coincidence that Winston Churchill once lived in one of the flats above the shop. Sautter is noted for his knowledge of Havanas in particular, and keeps a collection of rare and vintage cigars (not for sale) on the premises.

OTHER SHOPS

There are many other fine cigar shops in London, such as Shervingtons in High Holborn, the Segar and Snuff Parlour in Covent Garden, Tomtom in Belgravia and Wards in Gresham Street in the City. Outside London, outstanding retailers include Frederick Tranter of Bath, and there are good shops in many major cities such as Nottingham, Birmingham, Edinburgh and Leeds.

The advantage of buying cigars, particularly Havanas, from leading merchants in Britain is that quality control is stringent compared with many other parts of Europe. The disadvantage is that British import taxes are high, and tobacco taxes amongst the highest in the world. The cigars don't come cheap, but at least you can usually trust what you are buying.

GENEVA

Other major centres of the cigar trade in Europe include Paris and Geneva. In Geneva, there is the original Davidoff shop, on the Rue de Rive, founded during the Second World War. It is said that, after being deposed in the 1950s, King Farouk of Egypt once ordered 40,000 Hoyo de Monterrey Double Coronas from the shop – complete with personalized bands.

You will also find Gérard Père et Fils, a shop which only deals in fine Havanas, perfectly stored and subjected to strict quality control. The Gérards also published their own Havana cigar handbook a few years ago. For an expensive country, cigar prices in Switzerland are surprisingly reasonable.

PARIS

Here you can also find good cigar shops such as La Civette (157 rue Saint-Honoré), fairly low tobacco taxes and a thriving cigar culture. The Diplomaticos range of Havana cigars was created for the French government tobacco monopoly, Seita, in 1966. These are essentially Montecristos with a different label – and considerably cheaper. If you see them, buy them – but don't confuse them with the Dominican brand Licenciados, which has a similar label and band, featuring a carriage and scroll design.

SPAIN

As might be expected, given its historical connections with Cuba, Spain imports more cigars than anywhere else in Europe (the Spanish market for Havanas is around six times as big as the British one).

Prices are as low as you will find, but there are many machine-mades on sale, and the quality of the Havanas available is sometimes inferior and inconsistent – not surprising, perhaps, in such a captive market. There are also a number of local handmade brands, following in the great Spanish tradition, few of which find their way abroad, despite decent quality. Good shops include Gimeno in Barcelona.

GERMANY AND ITALY

There is an old tradition of cigar manufacture in Germany (machine-mades) and you'll find reputable shops in Hamburg, Berlin, Cologne and Munich. Italy is famous for its distinctive strong (and rather bitter) Toscani brand. But there are fewer top-quality cigar shops than one might expect, though Sincato in Rome has a big, well-stored selection. As in Spain, it's wise to check what you are buying carefully.

CANADA AND HONG KONG

Canada has major links with Cuba, particularly in tourism. Big selections of Cuban and non-Cuban cigars (at high prices thanks to tobacco tax) can be found in shops in Toronto, Vancouver and Halifax, Nova Scotia, where the firm of MacDonald Tobacco also organizes regular cigar dinners.

Hong Kong is also somewhere you can find decent cigars.

THE UNITED STATES

There are high-quality cigar stores throughout the United States, although, of course, they don't stock Havanas. One of the most famous is Nat Sherman at 500 Fifth Avenue in New York. All is dark mahogany, and you can find any accessory you might need.

The shop was founded in the 1930s, but, under Joel Sherman, moves with the times, with a web site and a number of own-brand Selections, mostly made in the Dominican Republic, but also in Honduras and Jamaica. This is one of the world's great cigar businesses, catering for all tastes and pockets, with over a million cigars on the premises. New York also boasts an ultra-modern Davidoff shop on Madison Avenue. There is also a branch of Davidoff in Beverly Hills, as well as an Alfred Dunhill outlet. In Washington

D.C., you should visit Georgetown Tobacco, ably run by David Berkebile.

CUBA

And what about Cuba? Havana cigars are obviously cheaper here than anywhere else. But don't get greedy: only buy cigars at recognized state-run outlets (including the airport, where the prices are the same as in official shops), otherwise you will have no idea what you are getting, and will most likely end up with rubbish.

Whatever you do, don't buy cigars on the street, however tempted you might be. To quote a telling tale: the London importers, Hunters and Frankau, were sent a box purporting to be Cohiba Robustos at the end of 1998. The box had been sent to its owner as a gift from a friend who had bought it in Havana.

On first inspection, it seemed fine. The box looked authentic – with all the stamps and stickers in place, other than the fact that there was no factory mark, something which can occasionally be omitted, even on genuine boxes. The two cigars left in the box also looked OK. But on closer inspection, it soon became clear that all was not what it seemed.

The ribbon wrapping the cigars was badly printed and of the wrong type. One of the cigars had a genuine band, the other had one which had been run off on a colour photocopier. One of them turned out to have filler leaves of the same type (no blend of *ligero*, *seco* and *volado*); the other was rock hard and filled with shreds of tobacco. They were certainly not Cohibas, and not even good cigars.

So, always beware of apparent bargains – in 'sales' for instance. You might well be buying machine-made versions of famous Havana brands, or non-Cuban cigars with the same names. There's no substitute for inspecting the box carefully.

The same applies at airports, where duty-free prices can seem very attractive – until you check the product. Cigars at airports are all too often poorly stored, and frequently old without the benefit of maturity that age can bring.

However, there are good airport shops at Heathrow, Geneva, in the Middle East, and elsewhere. The airport in Santo Domingo, in the Dominican Republic, carries a wide selection of locally-made cigars.

SMALL RETAILERS

Try to avoid buying cigars at small tobacco shops and newsagents. The cigars on offer will usually be old, because of low turnover, and badly stored. Having said that, wine shop chains, such as Oddbins in Britain, are taking cigars increasingly seriously, and sell well-stored cigars. The chain has more than 230 shops, and one of the latest to open, in Battersea, south London, actually has a humidor room.

Think twice before buying cigars in fancy packaging, such as 8-9-8, polished boxes, and, particularly, cigar shops' own brand boxes: you are paying extra for the packaging, and are better off buying the cigars loose.

Likewise think twice before buying single cigars in aluminium and (sometimes) glass tubes. Remember that some brands are sold at premium prices – where you are paying for the name and marketing costs, just as much as for quality. Cohibas, for instance, are premiumed at a whopping 50 per cent, and Montecristos at 15 per cent.

BUYING A FEW

If you only want to buy a few handmade cigars, try to get them either loose or in cedar boxes – usually ten or 25, depending on their size – rather than in small cartons of five. And, unless you have very good storage facilities (a humidor, for instance) only buy enough for the next month or two.

Above all, once you find a reliable and congenial cigar merchant, don't be afraid to ask for advice and to follow suggestions as to which brands and sizes are smoking particularly well at the time.

STORING CIGARS

*You've decided which cigars you like,
and you know what range of brands and
sizes you want to keep at home. Now it is
essential to make sure that they are
properly stored. I can't stress this too much.*

CIGARS, as natural products,
continue to mature
and ferment in their
cedar boxes if they are
well stored. This ageing
process resembles the
maturing of wine in a
cellar. But it needs help
from you. A badly-stored
cigar will be ruined, whilst a
carefully-stored one will get
better.

BASICS

Even if you don't have a humidor or a similar facility, make sure that your cigars aren't exposed to extremes of temperature. This is difficult with modern central heating and air-conditioning. If in doubt, keep them in the coolest part of the house. Ensure that the cedar boxes are stored in an airtight box, or cupboard.

The storage space should, ideally, have a humid atmosphere (65-70 per cent humidity), and be kept at a temperature of 65-70F. If you don't have sophisticated storage facilities, only buy cigars in relatively small numbers and try putting a damp sponge in the box or cupboard. You could also try putting a small glass of water in your storage box or cupboard. Or you could put the cedar boxes in polythene bags, spraying a small amount of water on to the inner surface of the bags. Then seal the bags.

Whatever method you use, check the cigars regularly. It's essential to make sure that the cigars don't dry out. But nor should cigars be kept in very damp conditions – which can lead to the development of mould and rotting.

AIRTIGHT BAG

A few cigar experts suggest that you store cigars in an airtight bag in the salad compartment of your refrigerator. However, most authorities warn that this is a risky method. If you try it, make sure that as much air as possible is expelled before you seal the bag. Take cigars out of the refrigerator well before you want to smoke them (at least half an hour) so that they can return to room temperature.

SMALL HUMIDIFIERS

You might consider buying a small humidifier (there are many types, available from major cigar shops, normally containing sponge or chalk which has to be suitably moistened) to put into the cedar box. You will have to remove a couple of cigars to fit it in.

HUMIDORS

The best option, though, is to buy a humidor. There are a great many different types and sizes on the market, so you should easily be able to find one to suit your pocket, your decorative tastes, and your smoking habits. Even if you have a humidor, you still have to monitor the health of your cigars, and to top-up the water in the humidor as required. Use distilled water if you can, as normal tap water will leave mineral deposits which will impair the humidor's efficiency. Make sure you put it in a suitable place (not next to a radiator) – your humidor will only control the humidity, not the temperature.

If your cigars are stored in unusually cold conditions, you will have to raise the humidity to compensate. You should never store cigars

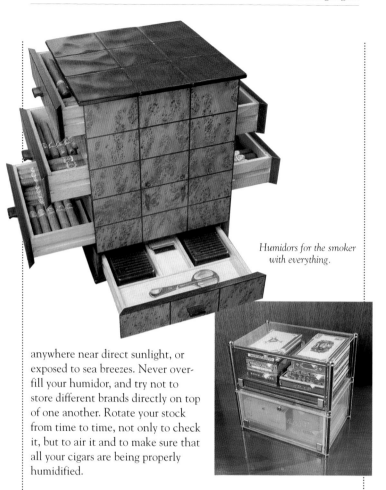

Humidors for the smoker with everything.

anywhere near direct sunlight, or exposed to sea breezes. Never over-fill your humidor, and try not to store different brands directly on top of one another. Rotate your stock from time to time, not only to check it, but to air it and to make sure that all your cigars are being properly humidified.

HUMIDOR ROOM

If you decide to convert a closet into a humidor room, make sure that humidity doesn't go above 75 per cent. The room shouldn't be completely airtight: a little air flow is essential to the health of cigars. As for shelving, it should be slatted wood (not solid), so that moisture can get to all your cedar boxes. The wooden shelves should also be sealed, otherwise they will absorb the moisture destined for your cigars.

PESTS

In hot climates, bugs can appear in cigars – weevils or tobacco beetles, for instance. The bugs lay their eggs in the tobacco, and their larvae eat it, leaving holes, and rendering the cigars useless. If you live in a hot country, this is something you will have to worry about.

Responsible importers in most countries take care to check for this; it's risky to store cigars from suppliers you don't trust.

Most leading cigar merchants will keep your stock of cigars for you, in perfect condition, particularly if you buy in reasonable, but by no means huge quantities. You can have a keep at James J. Fox and Robert Lewis, for instance, if you buy ten boxes.

MATURING CIGARS

Full-bodied cigars, specially those with big ring gauges, tend to age better than milder ones. But I should point out that some of the top full-bodied brands, such as Cohiba and Montecristo, won't particularly improve with age – apart from, possibly, the very largest sizes – because the tobacco is fermented longer in the first place, reducing the chances of any noticeable further maturation.

Wrappers which are likely to age well start off dark and oily, and get slightly darker and oilier as they mature. Milder cigars, particularly those with pale wrappers, will simply tend to lose their bouquet if they are kept too long. So smoke your light, mild cigars before dark, full-bodied ones.

Most major importers of top handmade brands make efforts to age them a little before releasing them to the public – a period of about two years for Havana cigars imported into Britain, for example.

But there is no strict rule about how long cigars should be left to mature and, as with wine, it can often be a matter of luck – though not if cigars aren't properly stored. Some experts consider that ageing cigars for six to ten years is the ideal. Others warn that even if they are stored under the best conditions, most cigars will lose their bouquet over this period. Anything but the best, and carefully monitored, storage also risks a gradual drying out. Most people in the cigar trade suggest that you smoke your cigars within ten years, and certainly that you shouldn't keep them beyond 15. However well stored, they're unlikely to get noticeably better after that time, and will continue to lose their bouquet.

There are even those who argue that if tobacco has been properly fermented, it is very unlikely to mature further after the cigars come on to the market for sale. If tobacco leaf has been fermented too little, of course, it can't mature at all.

You should smoke handmade cigars either within three months of manufacture or leave them for at least a year after they are made. The intervening 'period of sickness' as it is known – when the maturing process starts – is the worst time to smoke a high-quality cigar.

Don't imagine you can mature cigars particularly well in a table-top humidor, unless you are willing to devote considerable care to the task. Leave the job to a reputable cigar merchant, with whom you have a good relationship.

An open box of dried-out cigars can be revived in a polythene bag – see below.

The bad news is that if cigars are seriously dry, reviving them will be difficult, if not impossible. The good news is that semi-dry cigars can be revived, and that very dry cigars can still be smokeable, though as shadows of their former selves.

The key is to do things slowly and patiently. In theory, if moisture can escape from a cigar, it can also be replaced – though you shouldn't expect aroma and flavour to be as good as it once was.

The task of reviving cigars has to be undertaken slowly because the various parts of the cigar (wrapper, binder and filler) will absorb moisture at different rates. If rehydration of a cigar is too fast, you will risk it falling apart. Cigars lose moisture slowly, and can only regain it properly in the same way.

One of the simplest methods of reviving cigars which aren't too far gone is to put the open box of cigars in a large polythene bag, which is partially, but not completely, closed (you need to have a little air flow). Place a glass of water or a moist sponge in the bag. Rotate the cigars every few days, not forgetting to bring cigars from the bottom of the box to the top. With luck, the cigars should return to decent condition within three weeks or so. But it is a matter of trial and error and, above all, remember you will have to monitor the cigars carefully. There's no substitute for storing them well in the first place, as they will never be quite as good, even if successfully revived, as they were when you bought them.

You can also try to revive your cigars in a humidor. Start by putting the cigars as far away as possible from the humidifier, and then gradually move them closer over a period of weeks.

If you are a regular customer of a leading cigar shop, they will usually take pleasure in reviving your cigars for you in their humidor room – if they aren't too far gone. It will take around a month. If you have a good relationship with the shop, there is normally no charge for this service.

TRAVELLING WITH CIGARS

Travelling is potentially hazardous to cigars.
Apart from the mechanical knocks and the possibility of
having to open a box for customs, they will also be exposed
to changing temperatures and the drying effects of air-
conditioning and central heating in aircraft and hotel rooms.

TRAVEL HUMIDORS

IF YOU TRAVEL much with cigars, consider buying one of the many travel humidors on the market. They range from boxes which can be packed in carry-on luggage, to specially designed briefcases, to humidors with handles. But, whatever you do, don't put your travelling humidor or box of cigars in your suitcase, particularly if you are flying. That would be asking for trouble: huge temperature variations and mechanical knocks to name just two.

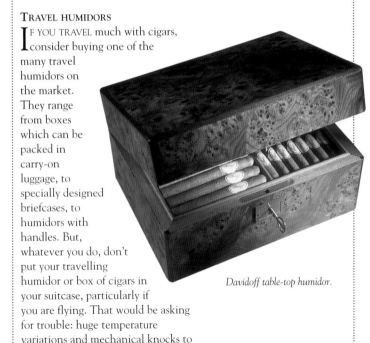

Davidoff table-top humidor.

POCKET CASE

If you are only travelling for a day or two, think about buying a pocket cigar case to fit the size and number of cigars you are likely to smoke. If it's in a coat pocket, beware of hanging up the coat near a radiator or other heat source – this can ruin the cigars.

Don't forget to take the cigars out of the case and return them to their box, or your humidor, when you get home. If you decide to use a travelling humidor, you should, equally, make sure that it is well away from direct sources of heat. So keep it in the wardrobe, or clothes cupboard, for instance.

SEALABLE BAGS

Most cigar merchants and importers use sealable heavy polythene bags (Zip Lock is one type) when they sell cigars to customers. These come in very useful if you are travelling with cigars. Keep the cedar cigar box in the bag, and put a slightly damp sponge in the bag (or spray the inside of the bag with a little water). Make sure your box is well padded by books or clothes so that it doesn't get knocked about. It should also be kept shut – use a rubber band.

FIRST AID

A simple way of reversing short-term deterioration after travelling (particularly if cigars have suffered air-conditioning on a plane or in a hotel room), is to turn the box upside down and put it under a gently running tap. Don't overdo it: just moisten the bottom of the box slightly. A sponge or a face flannel can also come in handy as an alternative method of dampening the bottom of the box. Shake off excess water and put the box in an airtight bag. Your cigars should get back to normal after a day or two.

CIGAR
ACCESSORIES

*The 1990s boom in cigar smoking has also led to the
marketing of a staggering range of cigar accessories:
cutters, lighters, ashtrays, cases and humidors.
What you pay for them depends, normally,
on the quality of craftsmanship and materials.
It's entirely up to you, but don't imagine that a very
expensive cutter or lighter is going to be any better at its job
than a mid-range one – though it may look more elegant.*

CUTTERS

Gcutters can be
round, square or oblong
in shape. They range
from plastic versions,
costing hardly anything
(those at Davidoff in
London cost £4.50), and
are often given away free by cigar merchants, to those
made of precious metals. Some of these upmarket
cutters are lacquered.

Left, *Cohiba, and*
right, *Harrods
cutters. The
Cohiba by
Dupont, is
finished in
Chinese
lacquer.*

Davidoff cutter.

At J.J. Fox and Robert Lewis, for
instance, alloy cutters (available in
six colours) go for £45, whilst a gold-
plated S.T. Dupont cutter, with a
Chinese lacquer finish, sells for £199.
At Davidoff in London, they sell stain-
less steel scissors with gold-plated handles for
£320, mid-range guillotines for around £60, and gold-
plated ones (with a pouch or key ring attachment) for £200.

Unless you buy the cheapest guillotine cutters, try to get those from
which you can easily remove shreds of tobacco, and whose blades you
can either get replaced or resharpened. Major cigar retailers will send
cutters back to the manufacturers for this purpose.

LIGHTERS

Cigar lighters, like cutters, come in many forms,
most of them expensive. At Davidoff, you can
buy silver-plated ones for £195, and you can get
special Davidoff lighters with double flames,
made by Dupont, for between £200 and £280 –
depending on the finish, which includes silver
and gold plating. A gold-plated pocket lighter,
with Chinese lacquer in the Maduro range
(made by Dupont) available at J.J. Fox and
Robert Lewis will set you back £495, with a
table lighter from the same range retailing at
£1,795. The shop also sells a sterling silver
match box for £135. Other match holders come
in mahogany and leather. Apart from Dupont,
leading manufacturers of accessories include
Dunhill, Ronson, Cartier, Colibri and Peterson.
Some firms have now started to produce
combined lighters and cutters.

HUMIDORS
(See also pages 132-133).
Humidors can cost from
under £100 to many
thousands. They are normally
made of wood such as
mahogany, walnut and
rosewood, as well as cedar.
There are also plastic, acrylic
and plexiglas models on the
market. They are available in a
variety of shapes and sizes and
can accommodate from 50 to a
couple of thousand cigars. You
will need one if you keep a
large stock of cigars (unless
you have alternative storage
facilities). If you only buy a
few cigars at a time and
smoke irregularly, you
probably won't.

Decide if you want to
pay for a fancy piece of
furniture (there's no need
to) or something more
functional. And buy one

Humidor marketed by the Nicolas Feuillatte champagne house, price £6,000 (US$6,500).

that suits the number of cigars and sizes you are likely to want to
store. It's best to buy one with trays at different levels: this allows you
to store various brands and sizes separately, and to rotate the cigars
from one tray to another as necessary. If you mix brands, you risk
mixing aromas as well – which somewhat defeats the object of
careful storage.

Basic humidors come from around £80 (Davidoff of London's
cheapest humidor, an acrylic model, houses 50 cigars and costs £125).
The cheapest types come with a strip which has to be regularly
moistened with distilled water. But you should probably expect to pay
around £200-£300 for a decent self-regulating humidor, the price
depending on the materials used in its construction and its capacity.

Expect to pay at least £500 for wooden humidors which can take up
to 100 cigars, and over £1,000 for boxes which can take more. You
can easily pay over double these sums for humidors with particularly
smart finishes. Some of the more expensive humidors come with two
humidity units. The most expensive humidor sold at Davidoff, in
London, goes for around £2,500, is made of mahogany and can store
up to 200 cigars.

You can also buy limited-edition humidors, and those made by well-known designers. The limited edition of only ten humidors designed by Guy Mallison for the Havana Club in London, for instance, holding up to 75 double coronas, were crafted in sycamore and ebony, and cost £2,200. Fox and Lewis sell humidors adapted from Victorian writing and jewellery boxes. Prices start at £700. Dunhill does the same. You could also transform a similar box of your own by adding a cedar lining and a humidifier unit – or go to somewhere like the Havana Club and they will do it for you for prices starting at around £400.

The humidors mentioned above are essentially boxes, however expensive. But they can also be handcrafted cabinets, such as the Habanos S.A. Millennium humidors, or the one recently put on the market by the champagne house of Nicolas Feuillatte, retailing for around £6,000. It is almost 2 foot high, is made of rare Macassar wood from Madagascar, and has eight drawers capable of holding up to 200 cigars.

There are also amusing oddities such as the work of the British furniture maker Martin Lane, who created special humidors for Harrods' 150th anniversary celebration. Martin Lane also makes custom-built humidors (through Fox and Lewis), starting at £2,000. And Alfred Dunhill in London recently commissioned a humidor, holding 75 cigars, designed by David Linley (son of Princess Margaret) in the shape of Andrea Palladio's famous Villa Rotunda. Sale price? A mere £19,500.

Whatever the price, choose your humidor carefully. Many are ineffective, or need careful monitoring. Pay attention to the general quality of construction. Make sure that the lid, which should be heavy, closes tightly. Check if the humidor is self-regulating (there is often a hygrometer inside to monitor the humidity level). Wooden humidors should be unvarnished inside, preferably lined with cedar. Humidors need to have regular air flow: this can be produced by opening the lid from time to time, but also by very small holes in the bottom of the box, which you should look out for. Some humidors also have units for storing cigar cutters, scissors and matches – but these are by no means essential.

Small humidors made of wood, metal or leather are also available for travellers, and can normally fit into briefcases or other carry-on luggage. These can also be used for temporary storage, or to transfer cigars from shop to home, or home to office, for instance. Firms such as Davidoff also sell briefcases with special cigar and accessory compartments, with suitable humidifiers. The Ambassador travel humidor, produced by Zero Haliburton, is made of high-quality aluminium, holds up to 30 double coronas on three trays, has a brief-case type handle, and sells for about £550.

CIGAR CASES

A number of pocket cigar cases are available. Go for ones made of leather. Make sure that they are lined, or well finished, so that your cigars don't get tainted with the smell of leather. Davidoff sell black kid leather cases in various sizes, lined with metal for extra protection.

And J.J. Fox and Robert Lewis make sturdy Florentine leather cases starting from £30. Some cases come with small moisturizing units, but these aren't particularly effective, and aren't necessary if you are going to smoke your cigars within the next day or two. Consider the case's strength, the number of cigars you want to carry and whether you want to carry one size or a variety. Also think about how big your pockets are, and the effect on your appearance if the case is too bulky. You might need more than one type of case. I favour a rigid, expandable, telescope-type of leather case in which I can carry large or small cigars.

OTHER ACCESSORIES

Many non-essential accessories are also available, including ashtrays (some of them 'own brand', exclusive to the shops involved, others made for leading cigar brands). In Britain, a range of bone china ashtrays featuring labels from four leading Havana brands sells for £75; whilst you can get porcelain ashtrays with adjustable rests from Fox and Lewis for up to £135. You can also buy single cigar tubes in brass, gold, silver or lacquered; cigar rests; and even a Victorian-style velvet cigar cap, rather like a fez (to protect the hair from smoke) – introduced with the launch of the Cuaba brand, and selling for £39.95 in Britain.

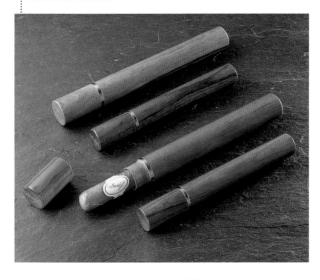

Davidoff cigar tubes.

COLLECTORS' ITEMS

Pre-Castro humidor made in Havana.

Cigars are now often a feature of sales at auction houses.
In London, at Christie's South Kensington branch,
cigars are frequently sold at wine sales (though in March
2000 there was one devoted exclusively to cigars).
At one of these, 200 cigar lots were auctioned, featuring
vintage or mature rarities. The cigars raised around
£400,000 – often at 50 per cent above the estimated price.

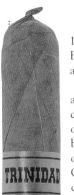

In late 1996, the businessman Peter de Savary bought 163 Havanas, made in 1857 and 1858 for the Duke of Buccleuch, for £17,600 at a Christie's sale – that's an average of £108 each.

Partly as a result of this sale, cigars, dating from 1864, also came on to the market from a store kept in an Irish country house, Temple House in Sligo. They were originally publicized as the remnants of a huge supply bought by a businessman when the bottom temporarily fell out of the Cuban cigar market as a result of the American Civil War. His descendant, Sandy Perceval, offered 600 cigars for sale altogether, with 500 of them in good condition, thanks to being kept in a humid cellar aided by the dampness of the west of Ireland climate. But despite the hype, experts later decided that the cigars, however ancient they might have been, actually came from the Philippines.

In May of the following year, a box of Trinidads (not then sold commercially) fetched £6,924 in Geneva. That means that each cigar in the box of 25 was worth £277 to the buyer. A few weeks later one of the 501 limited edition 1492 humidors made in 1992, to commemorate Columbus's voyage 500 years earlier, made £15,000, or £300 each for the 50 corona gorda cigars inside. The box originally sold for only £850. In November 1997, a box of 25 Trinidads (also sold in Geneva) made £9,890 – or £395 each.

Trinidad logo on inside of box lid.

Trinidad

PRE-REVOLUTIONARY HAVANAS

But these exceptions apart, the only serious collectors' market in cigars is in handmade pre-revolutionary Havanas. You can identify a pre-revolution box because the bottom of it will read in English: 'Made in Havana, Cuba'. A Spanish legend was only used after the revolution.

Prices for pre-revolution cigars, these days, can be as much as 400-500 per cent higher than those for equivalent modern cigars sold retail. London is one of the best places to find them, because of the tradition of keeping reserves at leading cigar merchants. They tend to come on to the market when someone dies, or when the owner realizes that he won't live long enough to smoke them all. American smokers are particularly keen on them because, apart from their rarity value, they can be bought with a clear conscience in the light of the United States embargo on Cuba.

The most keenly sought are sizes and brands which have otherwise disappeared. In May 1999, two boxes of five pre-revolutionary Hoyo de Monterrey 9 1/4 inch figurados, once owned by Hector Ayala, the last pre-revolutionary Cuban ambassador to France, went for a staggering £3,100 each – that's £620 per cigar. There is also a market in discontinued handmade Havana brands and sizes (some of them now machine-made) such as the Por Larranaga Magnum size, José Piedra and the famous La Excepción and José Gener marques.

The same applies to Havana Davidoffs and Dunhills – brands now made elsewhere. A box of 25 Cuban Davidoff Dom Perignons recently fetched over £5,000. With such high prices, it's not surprising that counterfeiters are also being inspired to produce their own versions of rare cigars: so, as always, be careful if you want to enter the collectors' market.

A GOOD SMOKE?

It's worth querying whether very old cigars are actually worth buying to smoke. As with very old fine wine, their viability is a matter of luck. If they have been properly stored, they might still be very good, but they can also be poor smokes, with little aroma or flavour – however excellent they might once have been. As a rule, you should avoid cigars made before the 1950s, and favour the darkest ones you can find.

There really is no collectors' market worth talking about in non-Havana cigars.

COLLECTABLE ACCESSORIES

But it isn't only the cigars themselves that have become collectors' items or can command high prices. There is also a burgeoning market for accessories, particularly those associated with famous smokers, or those which are very old or well crafted.

In 1998, for instance, a nine-carat gold cigar case given to Winston Churchill by Aristotle Onassis as a birthday present in 1960, was sold to a private collector for £43,300 at Sotheby's – as against an estimate of £15,000. The inscription read: 'Happy Birthday from Ari'. And a mundane typed letter inviting an MP for lunch sold for £3,000, because it was framed with one of Churchill's cigars. In an earlier sale, a battered single-cigar case, used by Churchill when he was a soldier on the Western Front in The First World War, fetched £4,830.

CASTRO'S SIGNATURE

Fidel Castro's signature also seems to sell. From 1993 to 1997, cigar boxes signed by him raised around a million dollars for the Medical Aid for Cuba Appeal. The first box he signed during this period was for the launch of the Cohiba Siglo series in London in 1993: it raised £12,000. And at a dinner at London's Dorchester hotel in October 1995, boxes of 50 Trinidads and Cohiba Torpedos (a size not made commercially), each signed by Castro, fetched between £7,000 and £13,000 each.

The main event at this dinner, though, was the sale of one of a limited edition of 150 humidors made to celebrate the 150th anniversary of the Partagas factory. Containing 150 cigars (Series D No. 4s, 8-9-8s and Lusitanias with old-style pointed heads), the humidor went for £30,000. But during a dinner in Havana in February 1997, to celebrate the 30th anniversary of the founding of the Cohiba brand, Castro's autograph did even better. Six lots were auctioned: all humidors filled with Cohibas. The first three lots went for a total of $143,000. The fourth lot consisted of 45 specially-made humidors, each filled with the unique Robustos Especiales size, not commercially available, and each of them individually numbered. One of the boxes, which was presented to Castro, was signed by him there and then, and returned for sale. It went for $49,000. Another lot (a single 30th-anniversary humidor) went for $40,000; and the final lot – a Cohiba box with a gold lid, containing 90 cigars, and signed by Fidel, went for a staggering $130,000 – bought by Lebanese cigar dealer Mohammed Zeidan. One of the numbered humidors (without its contents) was subsequently sold at Christie's, South Kensington, for £10,925.

MILLENNIUM ITEMS

Special memorial ashtrays and other artefacts (such as the plates produced for the London launch of the Cohiba Siglo series at Claridges in 1993) are also of interest to collectors. The Millennium, for instance, led to the production of a number of commemorative items, which will doubtless become collectors' items in due course. These include special boxes of cigar selections and a chromium-plated

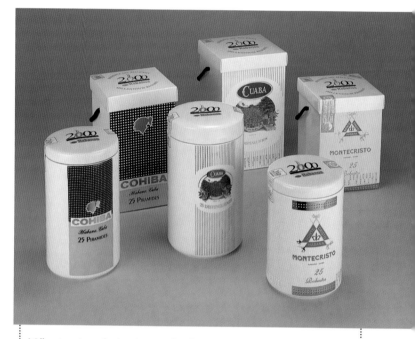

Millennium cigar selections in unusual packaging.

pocket cigar cutter produced by the London importers Hunters and Frankau; and Habanos S.A. produced 21 commemorative humidors at the beginning of 1999. Each humidor contained 2,000 cigars, selected from 20 Cuban brands, including sizes not on the market, or sizes which have not appeared for many years – such as the Partagas Salomon No. 2 ($6^3/8$ inches x 56 ring gauge) and the Punch Diademas Extra ($9^1/4$ inches x 47). The sale price for these handcrafted cedar cabinets, featuring a new humidifying system, was $100,000 dollars each.

Habanos also produced special limited editions of commercially unavailable cigars such as Cuaba Distinguidos ($6^3/8$ inches x 52), the Montecristo Robusto ($4^7/8$ inches x 50) and the Cohiba Piramide ($6^1/8$ inches x 52), all packed in ceramic jars of 25 cigars. The prices of these items are also likely to rise in the next few years.

The keenest collectors also go for cigar boxes of pre-revolutionary or extinct Cuban brands, as well as their bands. In the United States, there is a market for the bands and for richly decorative labels of the literally thousands of different types produced for domestic cigars in the 19th and early 20th century. Most of these labels sell for a few dollars, but the rarest can fetch several hundred.

THE
CIGAR
WORLD

THE CIGAR WORLD

Partido
Semivuelta   Havana
                        Oriente
Vuelta Abajo   CUBA   North Atlantic
          Pinar   Remedios   Ocean
          del
          Río   Caribbean Sea
                                        Oriente
                              Oriente

CUBA

CUBA WAS ONCE described
as 'a natural humidor', and
few would dispute that it produces the
finest cigar tobacco and, overall, the best cigars in the world. It is the
only country which can produce leaf of sufficient quality and variety
to make not only all the components of cigars, but also to allow
blending to achieve a wide range of flavours.

*Below, the most important area in Cuban leaf production (and the
only one that can technically give rise to 'Havana', as opposed to
'Cuban' cigars) is Vuelta Abajo in the lush Pinar del Río region at the
north-western end of the island. The semi-tropical climate and soil,
particularly in Vuelta Abajo, are perfect for cigar tobacco cultivation.*

VEGAS

Most of the tobacco is grown on small holdings, or *vegas*, ranging from five to 150 acres. Some of them are privately owned – including the famous Vegas Robaina plantation – but all of them sell tobacco, at a fixed price, only to the state-owned Cubatabaco monopoly. Some 100,000 acres are used for tobacco production in Pinar del Río. The plantations of the Vuelta Abajo, particularly those around the towns of San Juan y Martínez and San Luis, produce the very best Havana tobacco. In this small area, only some 5,000 acres produce filler and binder leaves, and about 2,500 acres are dedicated to growing wrapper leaves. Amongst the most famous *vegas* are Hoyo de Monterrey (for fillers) and El Corojo, for wrappers. Away from Pinar del Río province, high-quality wrappers are also produced in the Partido area, not far from Havana.

Apart from handmade Havanas, Cuba also produces many machine-made cigars and has a large domestic demand to satisfy, with around 300 million cigars produced, made of less good tobacco than those for export.

The Semivuelta area, to the south of Vuelta Abajo, is the second most important tobacco-growing part of Pinar del Río. The leaves produced there are thicker and have a stronger aroma than those from Vuelta Abajo. As a result, they are normally used only for domestic Cuban cigars.

Cigar tobacco is also grown in Oriente province, at the eastern end of the island, and in the Remedios (Vuelta Arriba) region in the middle of the country. But leaves from these areas are not of a quality deemed suitable for export.

THE GROWING MARKET

At the time of the Cuban revolution, some 44 million handmade cigars were produced for export, in more than a thousand different types (brands and sizes). This figure fell to 30 million shortly after the revolution. Rationalization of brands and sizes took place in 1979 and 1993. As a result, unusual sizes (such as the Por Larranaga Magnum) and brands such as José Gener, Gispert and José Piedra disappeared as handmades. The famous Cohiba brand, on the other hand, first appeared in 1966. The Havana Davidoff brand, created in 1969 as a flagship marque, ceased to be made in Cuba after 1990, following a dispute between Davidoff and Cubatabaco.

Unseasonal rain in 1991 and 1992, and storms in 1993, meant that handmade Havana production fell from 80 million in 1990 to only 50 million in 1994. This led to shortages, and a consequent rise in prices around the world. The same happened after 1980, when blue mould disease affected the Cuban tobacco crop.

But production rose again as the cigar boom took off, so that 86 million handmades were produced in 1997 (from around 59 million in 1996); in 1998, the figure topped over 100 million. Recognizing cigars as an essential source of foreign exchange, the Cubans are planning to produce even more in the future. New factories have opened, many of them outside Havana, with over 30 now in operation – double the figure that existed before the 1990s. And much more land is now devoted to tobacco production.

THE FUTURE

At the same time, some brands such as La Flor de Cano and Por Larranaga have been discontinued as handmades (though they are still made by machine). New marques, such as Vegas Robaina, Trinidad, and the all-figurado Cuaba, have, however, been introduced, and new sizes have been added to existing brands. The latest of these, San Cristóbal, was launched in November 1999. At the time of writing, 21 handmade Havana brands are available (though some of these have machine-made sizes as well). The big question, though, is what effect will this major increase in handmade production have on quality? The Cubans insist that strict quality control will be maintained, but others have their doubts.

An even bigger question is what will happen when the United States embargo on Cuba is eventually lifted, as most observers think it inevitably will be at some, not too distant, time. Apart from the enormous scope for acrimonious legal disputes over ownership of trademarks, such a change is also eventually likely to lead to a huge increase in demand for Havanas, as the American market legitimately opens up to the Cubans.

One can predict that it will lead to shortages and to an increase in prices. But how the Cubans will be able to cope, without reducing quality, is a question at the back of the minds of many Havana lovers. The Cubans have given assurances that supplies of suitable quality cigars will be maintained at present levels to their loyal old markets in Europe and elsewhere. But all bets are off, in my opinion, if normal market forces are allowed to operate – in terms of availability, quality and price.

COUNTERFEITS

Fake Havanas are already a major problem, and will doubtless abound in the future, particularly if the supply of genuine cigars fails to meet demand. To get an idea of the size of the trade in counterfeit cigars, you only have to know that late in 1999, a Dutch court ruled that a huge shipment of 75,000 cigars imported into The Netherlands, and purporting to be sought-after Havana brands, were actually all fakes. They could have flooded the European market, creating havoc. And that was just one shipment: the tip of a fast-growing iceberg.

HAVANA CIGARS
- WHAT TO BUY

There is something for everyone in the total range of Havana cigars available except, perhaps, for those who like very mild cigars.

The El Laguito factory.

COHIBA

COHIBA IS CURRENTLY the world's leading cigar brand, in terms of both prestige and price, though it remains to be seen if it will be superseded by Trinidad in due course. Founded in 1966, it was once – inaccurately – rumoured to have been Che Guevara's idea, but the man most responsible for its development and success was Avelino Lara, once a top-grade roller, and one of Cuba's greatest cigar experts. From 1968 to 1994, Lara ran the El Laguito factory, housed in a former mansion in a smart suburb of Havana. It is still very much the home of the Cohiba, although some sizes are also produced elsewhere, in the Partagas and H. Upmann factories, for instance. The name Cohiba itself has, at various times, been thought to be the Taino Indian word for cigar, smoking or tobacco: but nobody is quite certain which.

Cohibas were originally made to be given as exclusive gifts to foreign leaders and diplomats, often with personalized bands. The original box design bears no resemblance to the polished box, stamped with the head of a Taino Indian, found since the cigars went on general sale to mark the 1982 soccer World Cup in Spain. Supplies were limited at first, but Cohibas have been on general sale in most major countries (excluding the United States, of course) since the early 1990s.

The brand's origins are by no means clear-cut, but the currently accepted version of events is that cigars, privately made and blended by the roller Eduardo Rivera, came to the attention of Fidel Castro through one of his bodyguards. So impressed was Castro that he ordered official production of the cigars at El Laguito, and put Rivera in charge. The brand was designed to be the best available, but its distinctive flavour is not for everyone.

I frequently see people smoking Cohibas who would enjoy another brand more; others, who barely know how to smoke a cigar properly, seem to choose it for no other reason than that it is a status symbol.

Quality is paramount to Cohiba's makers, and the highest standards are strictly applied. Cohibas are made from the best leaves available ("the selection of the selection" as Lara liked to call them), taking priority over other brands; and they are made by the best rollers in Cuba. The key to the cigar's flavour is that the *ligero* and *seco* filler leaves used in its construction are fermented three times, rather than twice as with most other Havanas. This final fermentation – often taking as long as 18 months – takes place in barrels in the factory itself.

In 1966, the brand came in only three sizes, with three more added in 1989. Five more sizes, the Siglo series, were launched in London in November 1992, to celebrate the 500th anniversary of Columbus's great voyage. Cohibas are spicy and medium to full-bodied (the Siglo series is generally somewhat lighter than the earlier sizes). The Robusto is the richest, and a firm favourite with many seasoned smokers, followed by the Esplendido. Small sizes, such as the Panatela, which contain no ligero tobacco, are notably milder.

It has been argued that, because of the third fermentation, there is nothing to be gained by ageing Cohibas.

Cohibas made in the

Cohiba Panatela

Cohiba Robusto

Dominican Republic are produced for the United States market by General Cigar. As smokes, these bear no resemblance to the Cuban Cohibas. The typeface on their boxes and bands is the same as that used by Cuban Cohibas, but other elements of the packaging design are different. General Cigar originally started selling Dominican Cohibas in 1978, though they were only sold in a few stores in the United States. But the brand was completely repackaged, reblended and relaunched in 1997.

MONTECRISTO

This held the distinction of being the world's most prestigious and fashionable cigar brand before the official launch of Cohiba (and certainly after Davidoff cigars stopped being made in Cuba). Its export sales still easily beat those of other Havanas, indeed of all other Cuban brands put together, until recently. This huge demand has led to suspicions – refuted by the Cubans, but lingering nonetheless – that Montecristos in some markets (Spain, for instance) are not all that they might be. The popularity of the brand, and premium pricing, means that Montecristos are significantly more expensive than less illustrious Havanas.

The marque was founded by the Menendez and Garcia families in 1935 (Alexandre Dumas's novel *The Count of Monte Cristo* was once a favourite text read in Cuban factories – see page 68), originally available in limited quantities, and in only five sizes. At first, the Montecristo line was merely an offshoot of the H. Upmann brand, which the families had bought. The line was eventually established as a brand in its own right, with its distinctive crossed sword logo, at the behest of the British cigar importer John Hunter.

Cohiba Esplendido

The new brand first flourished in New York, particularly through the Dunhill shop. It only really took off in Britain and the rest of Europe after the Second World War. A new size (tubos) was also added at this time.

Seven more sizes were added to the range in the early 1970s, including the massive Montecristo A, weighing in at 9^{1}/4 inches (23 cm), with a ring gauge of 47 (a favourite with power smokers such as business tycoons and film stars) and Especial, with its twisted cap. Currently 11 sizes are available.

Montecristos, with simple brown and white bands, have a characteristically tangy, aromatic, medium to full flavour. The blend is attributed to the great cigar roller José Manuel Gonzalez, nicknamed Masinguilla ('the masseur') for his skill. They are tawny in colour, with slightly oily wrappers.

The No. 2, a piramide, is very full-bodied (with its 52 ring gauge), and I can recommend the No. 1, No. 3, and No. 4. The Montecristo A, and the No. 2 – which have a fourth type of leaf in their blend – are the only ones likely to age well. The Cubans produced a special reserve, a limited edition Robusto packed in a ceramic jar, for the Millennium.

The Menendez family moved to the Canary Islands after the Cuban revolution and launched the Montecruz brand (now made in the Dominican Republic) with a confusingly similar box and bands to Montecristo. Even more confusingly, in the mid-1990s, the Consolidated Cigar Corporation launched a Dominican line of Montecristos in the United States. These cigars have a very similar logo to Cuban Montecristos with 'M y G' (for Menendez and Garcia) where the word 'Habana' is found on the Cuban versions.

Montecristo Tubos

Montecristo No. 2

TRINIDAD

Officially launched in February 1998, Trinidad was once the rarest of Havanas, shrouded in mystery. The brand's existence was originally confirmed by a journalist who visited the El Laguito factory, until then famous for its Cohibas, in 1992. But nobody knows for sure who, exactly, was responsible for it originally. There were those who claimed it was Fidel Castro himself, to be given as a gift to foreign dignitaries when Cohibas

became available to the public. But Castro more or less denied that it was him in an interview in 1994. The French magazine, *L'Amateur de Cigare* later reported that the Cuban Foreign Ministry was responsible.

The Trinidads now on the market differ from those originally offered to the chosen few before their public launch. Those were considered too earthy and heavy by some who smoked them.

The cigar, still in one size (Fundador), is now slightly fatter with a 40 ring gauge rather than 38. The length remains $7^1/2$ inches (18.75 cm), but the blend has been changed to make Trinidads subtler, mellower and less rich.

They sell in boxes of 50 and 24. There are plans to launch a range, but these haven't come to fruition at the time of writing. Trinidads, as fine as they are, are very expensive and not for everyone. They come with gold bands simply printed with the brand name in black.

PARTAGAS

Partagas, founded in 1845 by Don Jaime Partagas, is one of the oldest Havana brands still on sale, and one of the best known. The old factory in Havana, near the Capitol building, has become a tourist attraction. There are over 40 types of Partagas, many of them machine-made (often with tell-tale cellophane wrapping). The brand was particularly popular in the 1920s and 1930s, and still has many devotees today among lovers of earthy full-bodied cigars with a pleasant aroma.

Go for the bigger sizes of Partagas – most of which are excellent – as some of the smaller ones are not very well made; and try to avoid the large numbers of machine-mades on the market.

The Lusitanias (a double corona) is well made with an excellent bouquet, and a slightly sweet, full flavour.

I also like the Churchill de Luxe. The Series D No. 4, a robusto with a distinctive band, typifies the qualities of the brand's bigger sizes, and though it has a strong and rather bitter aftertaste, it is a popular choice after a heavy meal for many experienced smokers.

The Selección Privada No. 1 (a long panatela) is very good.

The 8-9-8 , which is basically a Lonsdale, but slightly longer, is also recommended, as the Corona Grande (6 inches x 42), which also comes in 8-9-8 packaging. These two have a somewhat smoother flavour than the brand as a whole. The brand also features the unusual Culebras (twisted) cigar. Partagas cigars (which are darker than average, usually colorado claro, or colorado), age well.

There is also a Dominican version of the Partagas brand manufactured by General Cigar. Dominican Partagas carry the year 1845 on their bands, where the Cuban originals read 'Habana'.

Partagas
Series D No. 4

Below,
Partagas Culebras.

– 158 –

VEGAS ROBAINA

This is a new Havana brand, launched in 1997, and originally only available in Spain – though it is now more widely distributed (to the United Kingdom, for instance). It is named after Don Alejandro Robaina, probably Cuba's finest tobacco grower. He has been running the family plantations since 1950, in a tradition stretching back to the middle of the 19th century. Part of his success, and the reason for the quality of his leaf, is that he owns his plantation (unlike most in Cuba, which are state-owned) and thus keeps a highly experienced, and even legendary, eye on his plants. The filler is grown in Vuelta Abajo, the San Luis area in particular. The wrappers all come from the famous Vega Alejandro, particularly known for its high yields compared to other plantations. The cigars are made in the H. Upmann factory in Havana. At first, production difficulties caused a shortage of supplies.

These cigars haven't properly settled down at the time of writing, and it is difficult to give an accurate overall impression of the range. The larger ring gauge sizes seem oddly lighter than the smaller ones, and some of the cigars are medium to full, others light to medium. One of the problems has been that rollers, used in making other brands, have been making Robainas in an attempt to boost production, and the other is that, as such a new brand, a proper judgement can't be made until they've matured for another couple of years.

Try the Piramide-shaped Unicos or the Familiar (a corona). The latter is an excellent cigar, and notably spicy. The brand comes in five large sizes, all of them with ring gauges of 42 or over, and ranging from 5 inches to $7^{5}/8$th inches (12.5 to 19.3 cm) in length.

BOLIVAR

Although this famous brand was founded in 1901, it didn't really become as well known as it is today until after the Second World War. The name derives from the 19th-century South American revolutionary and liberator from Spanish rule, Simon Bolivar – whose portrait appears on both box and bands.

Bolivars are relatively cheap as Havanas go. They are very full-bodied, and not recommended for the beginner. An unusually high proportion of seco leaf in the filler blend is responsible for their flavour. Bolivars age well.

There are 19 handmade sizes in the range, but many of these are also made by machine – so, as always, check what you are buying. The larger sizes are favourites with experienced fans of heavy cigars. They have a powerful aroma, good draw, and better construction than the smaller sizes. The Belicosos Finos (torpedo-shaped) are popular after a heavy dinner; and the Royal Corona (a robusto) for a brief, smooth, but powerful smoke after a good lunch. There are also Dominican Bolivars on the market, with very similar packaging.

The brand once produced the smallest handmade Havana cigar, the Delgado, a corona measuring just under 2 inches (5 cm) with a ring gauge of 20.

H. UPMANN

H. Upmann is a brand steeped in history. In the first place, started in 1844, it is one of the oldest Cuban brands, founded by Herman Upmann, a banker who decided to diversify into cigars. And it is the brand responsible for introducing the cedar box in the form with which we are so familiar today. The firm was also responsible for the introduction of the cedar-lined aluminium tube in the 1930s. When the Upmann banking operation collapsed in 1922, the cigar side of the business was

Bolivar Belicosos Finos

taken over by the British firm of J. Frankau, who sold it to Menendez y Garcia in 1935. A new factory, which opened in central Havana nine years later to celebrate the brand's centenary, still produces H. Upmanns – though the Menendez and Garcia families eventually fled abroad after Castro came to power.

Upmann boxes feature the royal arms of the 19th-century Spanish King Alfonso XII, as well as coins alluding to the brand's banking origins.

Havana Upmanns offer a smooth mild to medium smoke, ideal for beginners or occasional smokers. But their construction sometimes lets them down, making them overheat. This may be a result of the many sizes available (more than 30), some of them almost identical. A handful of sizes are sold in tubes, as are some of the many machine-made Upmanns (which you should give a miss).

Dominican Upmanns with deceptively similar packaging to the Havanas are also to be found. The main difference is that non-Cuban labels, bands and tubes read: 'H.Upmann 1844', rather than 'H. Upmann Habana'.

ROMEO Y JULIETA

This is now among the most famous of Havana brands, but was originally founded in 1875 to produce cigars only for the Cuban domestic market. The brand's international success came thanks to 'Pepin' Rodriguez Fernandez. Formerly manager of another cigar factory, he resigned in 1903 and used his savings to buy the Romeo Y Julieta factory. Through his own tireless – not to say obsessive – efforts, and those of his staff (senior managers got a share of the profits), Romeo Y Julieta became the world's leading brand in just two years.

Romeo Y Julieta Churchill

As part of his marketing and promotional efforts, his factory at one time produced as many as 20,000 different bands to adorn the cigars of heads of state, celebrities and leading clients. Before he died in 1954, he named his biggest cigar in honour of Winston Churchill. He had earlier named cigars of the same size after the Prince of Wales (later Edward VII) and the French First World War leader, Georges Clemenceau. This medium-priced brand is particularly popular in Britain.

The range of Romeo Y Julieta cigars is vast: over 40 shapes and sizes, many of them available in aluminium tubes. There are also a large number of machine-made sizes to beware of. Many Romeo Y Julietas are excellent, classic cigars but, as always with such a big range, there will be those which some will find lacking. In general, the brand is mild to medium, though the Churchill sizes, with their gold bands (all the others, apart from the Cedro Deluxe series, have red bands) are fuller-flavoured with an impressive aroma – though you can't expect the tubed versions to be so well matured.

Cigars in the Cedro Deluxe series (wrapped in cedar) are all very good – but make sure the box or tube says 'de Luxe', otherwise you can be sure that you are actually buying machine-mades.

The Corona is also a good cigar; and the robusto sized Exhibición No. 4 is the choice of many connoisseurs for a satisfying smoke after a full meal. For small cigars (4 inches x 30), the Petit Julietas are surprisingly rich and well made.

There are also Dominican Republic and Honduras-made versions of Romeo Y Julieta, with similar band designs, but different text.

PUNCH

Punch is the second oldest Havana brand still in production, founded in 1840 by Manuel Lopez. It is also one of the best known and most widely available, with a huge range of sizes, many of them machine-made as well

as handmade, and mostly produced at the La Corona factory. Some of the many sizes (e.g. Palmas Reales and Exquistos) are only machine-made. The brand was originally aimed at the British market: hence the name, taken from the famous humorous magazine.

Punch cigars are mild to medium, and slightly sweet in flavour. At their best, they are very good, and have a notable bouquet and a spicy aroma. They are cheaper than many Havanas, and appeal to many beginners. Perhaps, as a result, they are disdained by some who ought to know better. They may have their reasons, however, in that with so many cigars in the range, quality is bound to waver. So stick to large sizes, such as the rich Punch (which ages well), Churchill and the Double Corona. It is worth noting that various sizes are given different names in different countries – just to confuse you.

There is also a Honduras Punch brand, but luckily, though the packaging (particularly aluminium tubes) is similar, the names of the cigars mostly differ from their Havana equivalents.

SAINT LUIS REY

These are full to very full-bodied, high-quality cigars, and one of my own favourite brands. The wrappers are smooth, oily and dark, but with a flavour much subtler than better-known full-bodied brands such as Partagas or Bolivar. And they have an excellent aroma. They are produced in small quantities at the Romeo Y Julieta factory (with only six sizes, three of which also come in machine-made versions).

Punch
Double Corona

The brand was created in the 1940s by British importers Nathan Silverstone and Michael de Keyser, and was named after the successful 1944 film version of Thornton Wilder's novel *The Bridge of San Luis Rey* – starring Akim Tamiroff and Alla Nazimova.

Don't confuse Saint Luis Reys with the San Luis Rey brand – made in Cuba for the German market, or the German mass-market machine-mades also called San Luis Rey. The Havanas have a mostly white box, with a red label. The cigars made for Germany have a black label.

RAMON ALLONES

The oldest Havana brand still in existence, founded in 1837. An immigrant to Cuba, from Galicia in Spain, Ramon Allones was the first cigar manufacturer to use lithographic labels to decorate cigar boxes. The brand's colourful boxes still brandish the Spanish royal coat of arms on a bright green background. The brand also pioneered the 8-9-8 form of packaging.

Ramon Allones (made in the Partagas factory since the 1920s) are the first choice of many keen smokers of full-bodied cigars, but are not recommended for novices. There is a small but interesting range of eight handmade sizes, most of which age very well. There are also a number of machine-made sizes (with names such as Mille Fleurs, Belvederes and Toppers) – to be avoided.

With their dark, high-quality wrappers, the cigars have a pronounced aroma, burn well and are well constructed. Their full flavour comes from a high proportion of ligero leaf in the filler blend (though smaller sizes are slightly milder).

Saint Luis
Rey Corona

Ramon Allones Specially Selected

Avoid the slim Ramonitas, but go for the 8-9-8 Churchill, the Specially Selected (a robusto) or Corona Gigantes for an intense smoke after a big meal.

Dominican Republic Ramon Allones also exist, with a similar band – though they are square, rather than round, and somewhat larger than those found on the Havana version. Their names are different.

Cuaba Tradicionales

Cuaba, one of the newest Cuban brands, returned to the old-fashioned figurado shape.

CUABA

These excellent mild to medium cigars were launched in London in autumn 1996, and are unusual in that the complete, but tiny, range of four sizes, are all figurados – tapered at the foot. Such cigars were commonplace in the 19th century, but were subsequently overtaken by straight-sided cigars (parejos). Now they are back in fashion again.

Cuabas are made in the Romeo Y Julieta factory. The name comes from the Taino Indian word for a bush plant (still found in Cuba) noted for its ability to burn easily. The various sizes are fairly similar (ring gauges go from 42 to 46, and lengths from 4 to 5⅝th inches).

RAFAEL GONZALEZ

Normally referred to as Rafael Gonzalez, rather than given their full name, Flor de Rafael Gonzalez, the brand is a favourite among discerning smokers, and has the added attraction of being sold at medium prices. They are very well made and burn well, and though mild to very mild, have a notably rich but subtle flavour, and a good aroma. With only nine cigars in the range, they have the aroma, in every sense, of class.

Rafael Gonzalez were originally created for the British market, and the box reads (in English): 'These cigars have been manufactured from a secret blend of pure Vuelta Abajo tobaccos selected by the Marquez Rafael Gonzalez, Grandee of Spain. For more than 20 years this brand has existed. In order that the connoisseur may fully appreciate the perfect fragrance, they should be smoked either within one month of the date of shipment from Havana or should be carefully matured for about one year.' A portrait of the great cigar lover, Lord Lonsdale, once adorned the inside of the lid, but no longer does so. The brown and white bands are very similar to those of Montecristo.

Try the Lonsdale or the equally good Corona Extra. Even the Cigarrito, with its very slim ring gauge of 26, is a good smoke. Beginners can do no better than start with this brand, and women smokers might well find the mild flavour and the elegant smaller cigars – with an unusually high quality for their size – very attractive.

Rafael Gonzalez
Lonsdale

– 166 –

HABANA · CUBA

HOYO DE MONTERREY

This famous mild brand was founded in 1865 by José Gener, a former leaf grower whose plantation outside the village of San Juan y Martínez in the Vuelta Abajo still produces some of the finest Havana binder and filler leaf to this day.

The brand used to specialize in large cigars, but in 1970, the Le Hoyo series of more 'accessible' cigars was added to the range. Hoyo de Monterreys are generally smooth, lightly fragrant and subtle – and too dull for some. The Le Hoyos are slightly spicier and fuller-bodied than the rest of the range.

The most famous Hoyo is the Double Corona. These large, rich but subtle cigars, made at the La Corona factory, were much sought after in the 1990s cigar boom. Shortage of supplies meant that connoisseurs were willing to go to inordinate lengths to get hold of them. They have a different band design to other Hoyos – much bigger and more flamboyant.

Other large sizes such as the Churchill and the huge Particulares (9 1/4 inches (23 cm x 47) have been dropped from the range. You should also try the Epicure No. 1 and No. 2 (robusto), if you like high-quality mild cigars. Hoyos don't age particularly well.

There is also a very good, but very different, Honduran version of Hoyo de Monterrey on the market. Their bands, although broadly similar in design, vary in small ways – no 'Habana', for instance – and they are maroon, not red and gold.

El Rey del Mundo

With production controlled by the Romeo Y Julieta factory, these are mild- to medium-flavoured cigars, chosen by many informed smokers. The brand, founded in 1882 by the firm of Antonio Allones, consists of subtle cigars with fine, oily wrappers. Even the bigger sizes are fairly mild, and good for after lunch or daytime smoking.

The range has been adjusted over the last few years with some sizes, such as the Tainos (Churchill) being discontinued. There are machine-made versions of some sizes, and Honduran versions with completely different names. They have similar bands, but substitute the word 'imported' for 'Habana'.

San Cristóbal

At the time of writing this is the newest Havana brand, launched in November 1999. Developed and produced by the La Corona factory, these very good rich, full-flavoured cigars have been given the original name of Cuba's capital – San Cristóbal de la Habana.

San Cristóbal come in just four sizes, each named after one of the forts that defended the city. Two of the sizes, La Fuerza ($5^1/2$ inches/13.75 cm x 50) and El Morro ($7^1/8$ inches (17.5 cm x 49) are entirely new and exclusive to the brand.

The newest Havana brand.

FONSECA

This brand, founded in 1891 by F.E. Fonseca, comes in only a few sizes, and it is not very well known outside Spain – where it is a great favourite among knowledgeable smokers. Fonsecas come individually wrapped in white tissue, with the box featuring both Havana's Morro castle and the Statue of Liberty – a throwback to the good old days before the U.S. embargo.

Fonsecas are light, mild to medium cigars with a somewhat salty flavour. Early in the 1990s, the Cubans seriously considered discontinuing their handmade Fonsecas in favour of machine-mades: but they changed their minds. Dominican versions of the brand have been on the market from as long ago as 1965. They have almost identical bands, but read 'Imported' where the Cuban versions say '*Habana*'.

LA GLORIA CUBANA

A brand with an old but chequered history, in that it was discontinued after the Cuban revolution, only to reappear in the 1970s to enlarge the range of cigars made at the Partagas factory. Then various sizes were shed in the late 1990s.

Rich, aromatic and peppery medium- to full-bodied cigars, La Gloria Cubanas are somewhat milder than Partagas. The Médaille D'Or part of the range comes in 8-9-8 varnished boxes. The other sizes come in regular boxes, and could well be phased out in due course.

There is also a very good version of the brand made in the Dominican Republic, and formerly produced in the United States. That the Dominican line recently introduced its own Médaille D'Or series only helps to confuse people.

Fonseca
Cosacos

La Gloria Cubana
Médaille D'Or 1

JUAN LOPEZ
Once only to
be found on
sale in Spain,
this very
mild, fragrant
brand isn't
easy to find, but
appeals to those
who can get hold of
it for daytime
smoking. The range of
names and sizes was
changed in the late
1990s. Look out for
the Selección No. 1
and No. 2.

Juan Lopez
Slimaranas

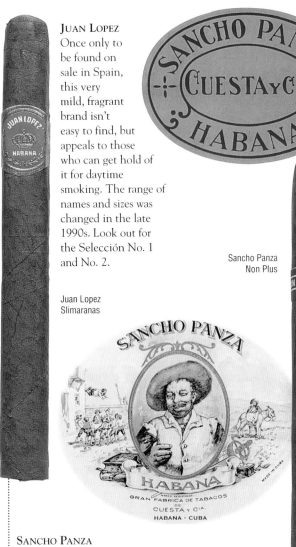

Sancho Panza
Non Plus

SANCHO PANZA
Good beginners' cigars, but not really for the seasoned
connoisseur. They are very mild, and some would say
subtle. Others find they lack flavour (apart from a slight
saltiness from time to time). They are very popular in
Spain. Even the largest sizes (including the Belicosos,
and the Montecristo A-sized Sanchos) are mild, but try
the Molino (a Lonsdale) or the well-constructed
Corona Gigantes. The brand became available in
Britain in the late 1990s.

Quintero
Panatala

QUINTERO

A good mild smoke, but not a particularly old or
distinguished brand. It was originally founded in the
1920s on the south coast of Cuba by Augustin Quintero
and, as such, didn't qualify as a Havana until 1940, when
the factory moved to the capital and Vuelta Abajo
tobacco started to be used.

It is now widely distributed, but many Quinteros are
machine-made, and widely distributed. Some Quinteros
come in 'hand-finished' versions. So check the box
carefully. Construction isn't always as good as it might
be, and you should note that the so-called Churchill is
really a Lonsdale.

DIPLOMATICOS

The Diplomaticos range, with a carriage and scrolls on
its band, was originally created for the French market in
1966. But the range is small, and availability is limited.
They are essentially Montecristos with a different label,
though this is sometimes denied, and as such they are
very high-quality cigars: rich and subtle. They are also cheaper than
the equivalent Montecristos. Don't confuse them with the Dominican
Republic brand Licenciados, which sports a
similar emblem.

A VISIT TO HAVANA

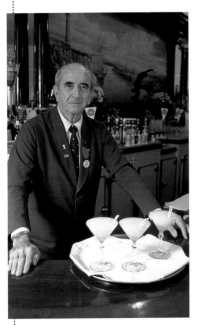

El Floridita.

Havana. *The very name is redolent of late nights and high living – cabarets, casinos and bars. Although much of that changed 40 years ago, when Castro and communism came to power and the Monte Carlo of the Caribbean had most of its corruption – and colour – squeezed out of it; but even now it is possible to visit the capital of Cuba and have a thoroughly good time – at least if you are a foreigner – in some of the most famous watering holes in the world.*

OLD HAVANA, now on the list of UNESCO 'heritage cities' thanks to its fine Spanish colonial architecture, mostly dates back to the 18th century. Here are some of the best and most famous bars in town. That they are so celebrated is thanks, in no small measure, to the presence in Cuba of Ernest Hemingway for a period stretching 30 years until his death in 1961. The legendary drinker (and, it's sometimes easy to forget, author) was, of course, associated with more than his share of bars around the world – but perhaps his favourite was El Floridita (353 Avenida de Belgica on the corner of Obispo).

Hemingway drank and smoked here – but is there anywhere he didn't?

EL FLORIDITA

In the heart of the former financial district of Old Havana this quintessential Havana bar is conveniently near the former Hotel Ambos Mundos, where 'Papa' used to stay before the Second World War. Like all bars in Cuba, it is now state-owned: but don't let that put you off. Refurbished a few years ago, it is, with its Empire decoration (dating from the early 19th century), murals of Havana harbour, and smartly liveried staff, as grand as anything you can find in Paris or New York. And the prices reflect that fact. As in most hotels and bars catering for foreigners, they charge in dollars.

But El Floridita's main claim to fame, and the reason it has attracted celebrities such as Spencer Tracy and Marlene Dietrich, is that it is, as an inscription under the bar announces, 'The Cradle of the Daiquiri'. Cradle, note, not birthplace – that was in the town of Santiago de Cuba, where someone thought of mixing Bacardi, sugar, maraschino, lime and grapefruit juice, and named it after the local mines.

The recipe, a far cry from the rather ridiculous concoctions often served in British and American cocktail bars, was overheard by barman Constantino Ribalaigua in the 1920s and perfected so that El Floridita, which Ribalaigua later owned, now serves no less than eight versions. The Hemingway Special is made without sugar – the way Papa preferred it when perched at the 40-foot (13-m) mahogany bar; and the way he drank it on the occasion when he set the record of downing 14 daiquiris, each with a double shot of rum, at one sitting. The famous Karsh portrait of Hemingway still hangs on the wall. English is widely spoken in El Floridita (they have menus in English) and, if you're hungry, the restaurant, though expensive, is among the best in a town not noted for its food.

Above, La Bodeguita. **Left,** El Patio.

La Bodeguita

When he wasn't propping up the bar at El Floridita, Hemingway would take the short stroll to La Bodeguita del Medio (207 Empedrado), a much scruffier but no less fashionable spot founded in 1942. With graffiti (they are happy for you to add your own contribution), photos and posters covering the wall, the place is reminiscent of a Parisian Left Bank bar, and indeed, tourists apart, is reputedly a haunt of artists, writers and intellectuals.

The bar itself is tiny, but has a small restaurant at the back serving reliable Creole specialities such as *picadillo a la habanera* (spiced beef) from its short menu. Entertainment is supplied – as in many Cuban bars and restaurants – by a guitar trio.

Intellectual companionship apart, La Bodeguita's main attraction for Hemingway, as it is for modern visitors, was its famous *mojito*. This refreshing cocktail of sugar, lime juice, rum, soda and angostura bitters garnished with a sprig of mint is expertly made at La Bodeguita. Behind the bar there is a handwritten endorsement from the Nobel prize-winning novelist himself:

> 'My *mojito* in La Bodeguita
> My *daiquiri* in El Floridita,'

it says, signed 'E. Hemingway'. La Bodeguita only serves various varieties of rum (the national drink, thanks to Cuba's sugar industry), and local Hatuey beer.

El Patio

Just around the corner from La Bodeguita, in the cathedral square, is El Patio, perhaps the prettiest, and certainly one of the best-situated bars in Havana. Hemingway didn't make it here, but only, one feels, because it didn't open until 1963, two years after he died. Dating from the 18th century, the house, with its arcaded portico and eponymous courtyard sporting a fountain, was once the home of the wealthy Marqués de Aguas Claras. Now the place boasts two restaurants and bars both inside and outdoors.

THE DOMINICAN REPUBLIC

The Dominican Republic is part of the island of Hispaniola (shared with Haiti) and lies south-east of Cuba. Since the island's north-western tip is no further than 60 miles from south-eastern Cuba, it has a similar climate, and, therefore, very good conditions for growing cigar tobacco.

CIBAO RIVER VALLEY

THE MAIN TOBACCO growing area is the 140-mile long Cibao River valley; and factories are centred around Santiago in the northern part of the country and La Romana on the south coast. Piloto Cubano tobacco (grown from Cuban seed) with its full aroma, and slow burning qualities, and Olor, which burns well and is slightly sweet, are two of the Dominican leaves most in demand.

Tobacco has been grown – and cigars have been made – in the Dominican Republic for many decades, but it is only over the last couple that the country has become a major exporter of premium cigars, rated by most connoisseurs as second only to Cuban.

The La Romana region of the Dominican Republic.

AMERICAN EXPORT

The main market for Dominican cigars is the United States. Exports to the U.S.A. rose from around five million in the mid-1970s, to over 30 million in the early 1980s – after the American companies General Cigar and Consolidated Cigar Corporation moved into production there. The Consolidated Cigar Corporation's La Romana factory, near the luxurious Casa de Campo resort, is one of the most advanced handmade cigar factories in the world, with the most modern quality control techniques.

BOOM TIME

At the start of the 1990s, export sales from the Dominican Republic expanded at a rate of around 5 per cent a year. But this figure boomed to 18 per cent in 1993 when 55 million handmade cigars were exported to the United States, just over half of the total number of handmades imported. Growth increased by an average of a further 20 per cent in 1994. This led to a shortage of tobacco to service the manufacture of top-quality cigars. But growth continued into the late 1990s.

Now the United States imports well over 100 million Dominican cigars annually. But the cigar boom of the 1990s also brought its own problems. The proliferation of cheap, badly-made 'Don Nobodies', with leaves that were not properly fermented, produced by as many as a hundred new factories which sprang up in the Santiago area, was no good to anyone. Now that the boom has levelled off, and the Don Nobodies have been exposed for what they are, the number of factories around Santiago has fallen to only 24.

Apart from making their own selections – some of them using the same names and livery as famous Cuban brands – the major Dominican factories also produce cigars for famous companies such as Dunhill and Davidoff, as well as 'own brands' for major cigar shops and distributors such as Nat Sherman, J.J. Fox and Robert Lewis, and J.R. Tobacco.

Until very recently, the tobacco grown in the Dominican Republic was mostly filler leaf, with wrappers, and often binders, imported from elsewhere. But the Fuente family has pioneered efforts to produce top-quality wrapper leaf in the country, a development likely to be emulated by others.

DOMINICAN CIGARS — WHAT TO BUY

Arturo Fuente
Reserva No. 2

Dominican cigars are, as a rule, notably cheaper than similar Havana handmades, but not all the brands listed below are widely distributed outside the United States. There are many brands and sizes, which will suit most tastes and pockets except for those looking for the finest full-bodied cigars. Below is a personal selection.

ARTURO FUENTE

Arturo
Fuente
Robusto

FUENTE IS ONE of the great names in Dominican cigar-making, with a commitment to the highest standards. The Fuentes have also done what was thought to be impossible: to produce high-quality wrapper leaves on their Château de la Fuente plantation near Caribe.

Arturo Fuente cigars are generally mild to medium, with the rich Fuente Opus X series (which carries much bigger and more ornate bands than other ranges in the brand) very much the flagship, wrapped in locally-grown leaf. Launched in 1995, this is a very popular cigar, but production is more limited than its fans would like.

Other Arturo Fuente lines are the Hemingway series of large figurados (the Masterpiece is 9 inches/22.5 cm x 52) and the standard range, mostly dressed with dark brown Cameroon wrappers; though some sizes also come in lighter Connecticut Shade. The Château Fuente (a robusto), encased in cedar, is a very good cigar.

Davidoff
Tubo
No. 2

Arturo Fuente
Château
Fuente

DAVIDOFF

The name Davidoff is virtually synonymous with cigars, and cigar shops – though it is now also linked to any number of accessories and items well beyond the world of smoking. It was in 1990 that Davidoff (by then a partnership between Zino Davidoff himself and Ernst Schneider's Swiss firm Öttinger) announced that there would be no further production in Cuba – where cigars bearing the name had been made since 1947. New factories were set up in Santiago.

Zino himself died in 1994, but the brand continues as one of the Dominican Republic's best known, and best made. Davidoffs are mild to medium in flavour (the Cuban versions were much richer) and made with Connecticut Shade wrappers and Dominican filler leaf.

Most Davidoffs are notably mild: the Nos. 1 and 2, and Ambassadrice, for instance. Even the large Aniversarios No. 1 and No. 2, produced to celebrate Zino Davidoff's 80th birthday, are remarkably mild for their size (8 2/3 inches/21.6 cm x 48, and 7 inches/ 17.5 cm x 48, respectively).

The Davidoff 1000 series is medium-flavoured; and the Gran Cru series is altogether richer. That also applies to the Davidoff Special R, a robusto with a wrapper leaf darker than that of the Gran Cru series, and the Special T (a piramide). The Double R is a double corona. Small machine-made Davidoffs are also produced in Europe: 'Davidoffs' only in name.

Davidoff 1000

Davidoff Special T

Davidoff Double R

DUNHILL

The old English firm of Alfred Dunhill is as well-known as Davidoff in the world of fine cigars – and has been for much longer. Today Dunhill, too, has branched out into realms far beyond that of the humble cigar.

Dunhill cigars are sold and marketed by the Rothmans International group of companies worldwide. There are three handmade ranges which can be found in various countries throughout the world; and there is also a machine-made line. Dunhill's flagship cigars – the Aged Cigar line – are made in the Dominican Republic.

There are 13 sizes of Aged Cigars, each made with Dominican Piloto, Olor and Brazil fillers, wrapped in Connecticut Shade leaf. Aged for a minimum of three months before they are distributed, they have blue and gold bands (the Dunhill logo was changed to its present script, from a more modern design, in 1995). They are well made and blended, burn evenly and have a medium to full flavour, without being too rich.

Dunhill Peravias

Dunhill Centenas

Dunhill Romanas

Avo XO Maestoso

AVO

Beirut-born Avo Uvezian is a musician and composer (he trained at the famous Julliard School of Music) and since he understands the importance of careful composition, all Avo cigars are well constructed. Both his standard line, and the seven cigars in the more recent XO Trio and Quartetto series, have high-quality Connecticut wrappers and Dominican fillers from the Cibao valley. The elegant XO series is more expensive than the rest of a brand, which is by no means cheap.

Avo flavours, based on aged Piloto Cubano filler tobacco, get richer as the cigars get bigger, and go from medium to full. The XO Intermezzo (a robusto, but longer than is traditional), Maestoso and Notturno are particularly successful. Sales since Uvezian started the firm in 1988 (it is now owned by Öttinger, parent company of Davidoff) have soared from a few thousand a year, sold only in Davidoff's New York store, to more than three million a year.

PAUL GARMIRIAN

Paul Garmirian's P.G. cigars are some of my favourite non-Havanas. Garmirian is a man of many talents. Based near Washington D.C., he has a Ph.D in international politics and

Paul Garmirian Belicoso

used to be a real-estate agent until the success of his brand, launched in 1991, led him to go into the cigar business full-time. His passion for cigars stretches back more than 30 years, and has established him as a leading expert on handmade cigars: a fact reflected in his book, *The Gourmet Guide to Cigars*. His cigars, once only available in limited quantities, are now widely available in the United States, as well as in two London stores.

Paul Garmirian cigars have dark, slightly oily, reddish mid-brown wrappers. They are very well constructed, burn well as a result, and have a subtle bouquet, and a mellow – though medium to full-bodied – flavour. P.G.s are excellent cigars, and, in my opinion, the Belicoso is the star of the line. The number of sizes available has now increased to 18.

PARTAGAS

The Dominican version of this great Cuban brand is made with Cameroon wrappers. Fillers are a mixture of Dominican and Mexican tobacco, and binders are from Mexico. There is a comprehensive range of sizes, quite a few of them numbered. They are very well made, smooth, slightly sweet, and medium to full-bodied. General Cigar are the brand's producers – originally they had the guidance of Benjamin Menendez and Ramon Cifuentes, of the famous Cuban cigar families.

The Dominican Partagas known as Limited Reserve are more expensive than the rest of the brand (which is not cheap), and come with green rather than red bands. The best of these Partagas are very good indeed, and, not surprisingly, very popular in the U.S.A.

RAMON ALLONES

Dominican Ramon Allones are produced by General Cigar. They have medium to dark Cameroon wrappers, Mexican binders and fillers blended from Dominican, Jamaican and Mexican tobacco. They are very well constructed, mild to medium in flavour and fairly expensive. The range is small, consisting entirely of cigars with medium to large ring gauges.

Partagas Limited Reserve Royale

H. UPMANN

Handmade cigars bearing the famous Cuban H. Upmann name are made by the Consolidated Cigar Corporation. With their Cameroon wrappers, they are well-made, mild to medium smokes, and very popular in the United States. The Chairman's Reserve series is more expensive than the rest of the brand, which is reasonably priced.

H. Upmann Lonsdale

H. Upmann Corona

H. Upmann Pequenos No.100

LA GLORIA CUBANA

The Gloria Cubana range was
founded in Miami by Ernesto
Carrillo, and was originally only
sold locally. But Carrillo, a man
dedicated to making fine cigars,
moved production to the
Dominican Republic in the
1990s. His excellent cigars are
medium to full-bodied, with dark
wrappers from Ecuador, and fillers
and binders from the Dominican
Republic, Brazil, Mexico and
Nicaragua and the fillers are a
blend of Dominican, Brazilian
and Mexican leaves.

Gloria Cubanas are very
attractive cigars, originally
available in only five sizes, all
with large ring gauges. Recently
11 new sizes have been added.
The larger sizes are still the best
in my opinion. Try the Wavell (a
robusto), the Churchill (7
inches/17.5 cm x 50), or the
Soberano (8 inches/20 cm x 52)
if you like rich cigars. The
original Havana Gloria Cubana
brand is still produced by
the Cubans.

ASHTON

A high-quality Dominican brand
which, though it has only existed
since 1985, has established itself
as a favourite with many who like
mild to medium cigars. There are a
number of lines, all manufactured by
the Fuente family, though the brand is
owned by a Philadelphia outfit.

The standard selection consists of nine
medium-flavoured sizes with Connecticut Shade wrappers
and Dominican and Brazilian filler leaf. The Cabinet
Selection (aged for a year) is somewhat smoother. As many
as six tobaccos are used for the line as a whole.

Ashton Cabinet No. 3

Ashton Cabinet No. 2

Ashton includes a number of figurados, which have more ornate bands than the simple white and yellow of the basic line.

The Aged Maduro line is dark and sweet, and uses Connecticut broadleaf (rather than Shade) wrappers.

The Ashton Crown series comes with Dominican wrappers from the Château de la Fuente plantation. I recommend the Magnum (robusto) size of the standard line: a good mild to medium, but aromatic, smoke.

Ashton Magnum

Cuesta-Rey Dominican No. 1

CUESTA-REY

A very old brand, founded in Tampa, Florida, in 1884 by Angel La Madrid Cuesta and Peregrino Rey. The firm was taken over by another old Tampa business, M&N, in 1958. The cigars were originally made in the United States. Production in the Dominican Republic began in the 1980s.

Cuesta-Reys are well-made, mild cigars and come in two handmade lines: the Cabinet Selection and the Centennial Vintage Collection. The former have dark Cameroon wrappers, the latter come in Connecticut Shade with a filler blend using four types of leaf. There are also machine-made Cuesta-Reys, but the handmades are labelled as such.

SANTA DAMIANA

Formerly a well-known Havana brand, Santa
Damiana cigars are now made at La
Romana by the Consolidated Cigar
Corporation. Santa Damianas destined
for the United States are lighter than,
and have different names and sizes from,
those available in Europe. Those sold in
America have numbers (Selección No.
100 etc.), whilst those on sale in Europe
have traditional names.

All Santa Damianas are well made,
with a delicate, slightly spicy flavour, and
a pleasing aroma. The brand as a whole
ranges from mild to medium, with a
blend consisting of Dominican and
Mexican filler. The binders come from
Mexico, and the wrappers are shade-
grown in Honduras.

Cuesta-Rey Captiva

Santa Damiana Selección 300

POR LARRANAGA

These are excellent cigars, using the
same name as the Havana brand which
was founded in 1834, and which has
very similar bands, but is now only
machine-made.

Por Larranagas are mild to medium,
but full of flavour, and are extremely
well made, with Connecticut Shade
wrappers, Dominican binders, and
fillers blended from Dominican and
Brazilian leaves.

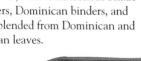

Por Larranaga Fabulosos

Agio's Balmoral.

BALMORAL

A new brand, not Scottish, as the name might suggest, but owned by Dutch cigar makers Agio – until now best known for their machine-mades. Balmoral are made in the town of San Pedro de Macorís, with Dominican filler, Brazilian binder and Ecuadorian, shade-grown wrappers. The name itself has been carried by Dutch cigars for more than a century.

The Royal Selection, as it is called, consists of five sizes of well-made, mild to medium cigars. They come individually wrapped in cellophane.

Griffin No. 300

GRIFFIN'S

This extremely well-constructed brand was founded by Swiss-based Bernard Grobett, an associate of Zino Davidoff.

Grobett was one of the first Europeans to start production in the Dominican Republic (in the 1980s), but Griffin's are now made and distributed by the Davidoff organization.

Griffin's are mild to medium, with pale Connecticut Shade wrappers, and Dominican filler. They have many devotees, but don't come cheap.

PLEIADES

A French-owned brand of mild but flavourful cigars. They look good and are well made. Filler leaves (Olor domicano and Piloto cubano) come from the Cibao valley. After they are manufactured (at Santiago de Los Caballeros), the cigars are transported to Strasbourg, where they are placed in boxes with a built-in humidifying system, before being distributed in Europe and the United States. They are named after planets and constellations.

The makers of Pleiades have now introduced a new brand, Cruzeros. These are handsome cigars, stylishly packaged, also from the Dominican Republic. They are, on the whole, fuller and richer than Pleiades (though the smaller ring gauge sizes are fairly mild), with a hint of spicy sweetness. Both Pleiades and Cruzeros come in an impressive range of sizes.

Pleiades Uranus

Pleiades Aldebran

– 189 –

PRIMO DEL REY

Made by the Consolidated Cigar Corporation in the Dominican Republic, these are mild to medium and very well made. They come in a large array of sizes, many of them with a choice of *claro* ('natural'), double *claro*, and *colorado* wrappers from Brazil. The bands look similar to Montecristo for most sizes, apart from the small Club Selection which has red and gold bands on a white background.

MONTECRISTO

In the mid-1990s, the Consolidated Cigar Corporation launched a Dominican line of Montecristos in the United States. These have a very similar logo to Cuban Montecristos with 'M y G' (for Menendez and Garcia) where the word '*Habana*' would be on the Cuban versions.

In the wake of a legal dispute, Consolidated has the rights to the brand name in the United States and a few other markets, with Tabacalera (the Spanish monopoly) owning it elsewhere. The cigars are medium-flavoured and well made with Dominican filler and Connecticut Shade wrappers.

PREMIUM DOMINICANA

A fairly new brand made to a blend developed by Carlos Fuente Sr. The wrappers are from Ecuador. These cigars are nicely aged, well made, and have a full flavour. The range consists only of large ring gauge cigars, appropriate to their characteristically rich taste.

Primo del Rey Regal

Henry Clay Breva Fina

HENRY CLAY

Originally a Havana brand, with a history stretching back to the 19th century (it was named after an American senator with Cuban connections). Production of the brand was switched to Trenton, New Jersey in the 1930s, but the cigars are now made in the Dominican Republic. Until recently, there were only three sizes, Breva Fina, Breva Conserva, and Breva – all medium to full-bodied, with mid-brown Connecticut broadleaf wrappers. Now Consolidated Cigar has added six new even fuller-bodied sizes with dark Cuban-seed wrappers from Nicaragua. The Cedro Deluxe comes wrapped in cedar. The Fantasias come in glass tubes. The Obelix is a piramide.

Henry Clay Breva Conserva

Henry Clay Breva

FONSECA

An old Cuban brand, which has been made in the Dominican Republic since 1965. These are very well-made, smooth, mild cigars, originally with Cameroon wrappers, but now dressed in Connecticut Shade. Binders come from Mexico, and fillers from the Dominican Republic. The range is small, concentrating on large ring gauges.

Fonseca No. 10-10

CASA BLANCA

This brand's speciality is huge cigars. I need only mention the Magnum, with a 60 ring gauge, and the Jeroboam and Half Jeroboam, both with massive 66 ring gauges, the former weighing in at 10 inches (25 cm). Though the range includes these oddities (which someone must buy), the cigars are well made, mild and smooth. Casa Blancas come in light Connecticut wrappers, with some sizes also available in *maduro*. Larger sizes are available in both claro (Connecticut) and maduro wrappers. The filler leaves come from the Dominican Republic, and binders are Mexican.

JUAN CLEMENTE

Founded in 1982 by Frenchman Jean Clement. These cigars come with a blend of Dominican Republic filler, and have Connecticut Shade wrappers. Construction has sometimes not been all it could be, but there have been recent signs of a considerable improvement. Juan Clementes are mild and fragrant (I particularly like the Rothschild). The Club Selection line, with darker wrappers, shows the brand at its mellow best. The range has been much extended since the brand was created, and is now very comprehensive. It includes the whopping Gargantua – 13 inches (32.5 cm) long, with a ring gauge of 50. The band on Juan Clementes is, uniquely, applied to the foot of the cigar rather than the head. Club Selection cigars have a white band, as against yellow for the rest of the brand.

Juan Clemente Club Selection No. 2

Juan Clemente Club Selection No. 3

V CENTENNIAL

Why V Centennial? Because the brand was launched to commemorate the fifth centenary of Columbus's voyage to the New World. The cigars, formerly made in Honduras, are now produced by Tropical Tobacco in a new 70,000-square-foot factory in the Dominican Republic, masterminded by Pedro Martin.

Wrappers are Connecticut Shade, binders Mexican, and the filler a mixture of spicy Honduran leaf, aromatic Nicaraguan leaf, and Dominican leaf. So these are complex cigars and, generally, the combination works very well. They are well constructed and come in large sizes. A couple of Perfectos have been added, and there is an unusually shaped Torpedo.

The cigars come in two lines: the standard selection, and the higher priced '500' series, with its distinctive logo and rich flavours. The Numero Dos of the 500 series recently gained a 92 (out of 100) rating from *Cigar Insider*, and the Robusto was given 90. The brand is medium to full-bodied.

BAUZA

Well-made, high-quality, aromatic mild to medium cigars, at competitive prices. Wrappers come from Ecuador, binders from Mexico, and the filler blend is composed of leaves from Nicaragua and the Dominican Republic.

Bauza Casa Grande

V Centennial Torpedo

HONDURAS

Honduras comes after the Dominican Republic as a major producer of handmade cigars, particularly as an exporter to the United States. The country, the second biggest in Central America, is mountainous, with a heavy rainfall. Cigar production is centred in three areas: Danlí, on the border with Nicaragua (to the south), Santa Rosa de Copán, near Guatemala (to the north), and San Pedro Sula, close to the Caribbean coast.

A S WITH THE DOMINICAN REPUBLIC, Honduras has been a centre of tobacco growing and cigar production since the 19th century, but has seen the industry only really take off in the late 1980s and 1990s. Factories and production methods are less modern than in the Dominican Republic, but the average turn-out per roller is high – prompting some to question quality control.

Dunhill Churchills, one of the brand's five sizes made in Honduras.

CUBAN SEED

A particular feature of Honduran cigars is that many are made from filler tobacco grown from Cuban seed. As a result, they are characteristically full-bodied, and manufacturers claim that they offer the nearest thing to Havana cigars to be made outside Cuba. But much of the leaf used is also from other countries, wrappers in particular, although shade-grown tobacco from Connecticut seed is also cultivated.

THE CLIMATE FACTOR

Honduras is particularly susceptible to heavy winds and rain which, over the years, have badly affected production, most recently Hurricane Mitch in 1998. The wet conditions have also led to infestations of blue mould disease, leading to a shift by some growers to the warmer, drier months of January and February, rather than November and December. Experts claim that Honduran leaf grown during these months is thicker and coarser than it might otherwise be – leading to cigars with a rougher flavour.

Excalibur No. IV

HONDURAN CIGARS — WHAT TO BUY

The best Honduran cigars are as good as any in the world, and often come at surprisingly reasonable prices – particularly those sold loose and unbanded. But don't expect a mild smoke, and look elsewhere if you are a beginner – unless you want to jump in at the deep end.

HOYO DE MONTERREY/EXCALIBUR

T HESE ARE GENERALLY very well-made cigars, with a strong flavour, and are available in a considerable range of sizes. In 1998, manufacturers Villazon brought out a new line, which they describe as the 'limited edition' Selección Royale, with labels similar to the Cuban Hoyo de Monterrey Double Corona.

There are four sizes at the time of writing: Duques (a pyramid), Aristocrat, Condesa, and Marques. They are described as 'figurados', but strictly, this term only applies to the Aristocrat.

The Excalibur series of Hoyos (fillers grown from Cuban seed; wrappers made of Connecticut Shade) are among the very best non-Havana medium- to full-bodied cigars on the market: rich and very well made, the brainchild of Villazon's Frank Llaneza. For trademark reasons, they are sold with the Hoyo de Monterrey label in the United States (with the additional word Excalibur at the bottom of the band), but simply as Excalibur in Europe.

Four new sizes of Excalibur have recently been added. Most of the line is designated by Roman numerals. New sizes include the Emperor (8^1/2 inches/21.25 cm x 52) and a couple of thin cigars: the No. VIII (5^1/4 inches/13 cm x 28) and Cigarillo (4 inches/10 cm x 24).

DON TOMAS

Very well-made cigars from U.S. Cigar, developed in 1973. They are available in three lines – all differently priced and medium to full-bodied. The standard series comes in maduro Indonesian wrappers (with Colombian binders and fillers of Cuban-seed tobacco from the Dominican Republic, Mexico and Nicaragua) in a range which has been reducd to eight sizes, including a 'Corona' with an unusually large ring gauge of 50.

The International series consists of only four numbered premium-priced sizes with Indonesian wrappers, Dominican binders and a filler blend from the Dominican Republic, Brazil and Indonesia. They are described as 'Cuban-styled'. Special Edition has five super-premium priced (numbered 100, 200 etc.) sizes now made using Indonesian Jember wrappers, Mexican binders, and filler leaves from the Dominican Republic and Mexico.

ZINO

This high-quality brand was created by the great Zino Davidoff for the American market when Davidoff cigars were still being produced in Cuba, and thus unavailable in the United States. The cigars come in two regular lines – neither of them cheap. The standard line (with gold bands) is medium-bodied. The mild but aromatic Mouton Cadet series, with its distinctive dark red band, was launched

Zino Mouton Cadet No. 6

Zino Veritas

Don Tomas Imperial

in the 1980s and promoted at the time by Baroness Phillipine de Rothschild, whose family produce the eponymous claret. The Connoisseur series was specially produced to celebrate the opening of the Davidoff shop in New York in 1987, and consists of fuller-bodied cigars with large ring gauges. You might come across Zinos machine-made in Holland using Indonesian and Brazilian tobacco. Don't confuse them with the real thing.

C.A.O.

C.A.O. International's Honduran cigars (the Black Label line) have been made since 1995 at Nestor Plasencia's former factory at Danlí, now sold to Tabacalera, S.A. of Spain. The filler tobaccos have changed slightly from the original blend – with Cuban seed tobacco from Nicaragua and ligero leaf from Mexican seed grown in Costa Rica. The binders are Dominican and wrappers are Connecticut Shade. These subtle changes have resulted in cigars which are similar to their predecessors but better constructed and have an improved flavour. They offer a mild smoke.

A new line, C.A.O. Gold, was so successful after its launch in 1996 that demand soon greatly exceeded supply. It is available in six sizes (a Torpedo, limited quantities only, was recently added) and the Double Corona received a 90 out of 100 rating in the October 1998 issue of *Cigar Aficionado*.

In 1998, C.A.O. launched an even better line, Aniversario, to celebrate the company's 30th anniversary in the tobacco industry. These are *maduro* cigars (the Honduran Black Label maduros have now been discontinued) made in Costa Rica in four sizes including a Belicoso. The wrappers are dark Connecticut broadleaf with Sumatran seed binders from Ecuador and Dominican and Nicaraguan filler. The cigars are aged for a minimum of 90 days. At the time of writing, C.A.O. were planning to change the name of this line. They are medium to full-bodied.

C.A.O. Corona Gorda

C.A.O. Corona Maduro

CASTANO

A recently-introduced brand with five sizes, all with large ring gauges. The cigars are generally well constructed, with Connecticut broadleaf binder, and quality Sumatra seed wrapper from Ecuador (both 'natural' and *maduro*). These are rich and spicy cigars – supposedly 'Cuban style' – which offer a decent smoke but are perhaps rolled rather too tightly to draw as well as they might. Try the Corona Especial.

DON RAMOS

Well-made, competitively priced, mellow, medium-bodied cigars made in San Pedro Sula of Honduran leaf and available in bundles, as well as boxes and aluminium tubes (in most sizes). The bundles are numbered, but the other forms of packaging and tubes carry names. The brand's band and tube designs were changed in the late 1990s.

PUNCH

The Honduran Punch brand, which started production as long ago as 1969, offers a range of more than 20 sizes of very well-made cigars. The standard line delivers a typically rich Honduran flavour (the filler blend is a mixture of Honduran, Nicaraguan and Dominican leaf; with Connecticut broadleaf binders and Sumatra seed wrappers from Ecuador). The Delux and Gran Cru lines offer more subtle pleasures. The Delux series is full-bodied, whilst

Punch Superiores Delux

Punch Britannia Delux

– 199 –

the Gran Cru line (with Honduran, Nicaraguan and Piloto Cubano filler, Ecuadorian binders and Connecticut Shade wrappers) is mild to medium and the flagship of the brand. There is a choice of wrapper colour (including *maduro*) in many sizes. A number of sizes are sold in tubes.

ASTRAL

A top-quality brand launched in 1995 by U.S. Cigar, and made in Danlí. The standard line of five sizes consists of smooth, mild to medium cigars made with Ecuadoran wrapper leaf (shade-grown from Connecticut seed tobacco), binders from the Dominican Republic, and a filler blend of leaves grown from Cuban seed in the Dominican Republic and Nicaragua.

The ring gauges are large, ranging from 44 to 52. The spicier (and pricier) Grand Reserve Vintage selection is fuller-bodied and more subtle, with well-aged Jember wrapper from Indonesia, binders from Mexico and filler leaves from the Dominican Republic (Piloto Cubano) and Mexico.

Punch Monarcas

Dunhill Robusto

DUNHILL

Dunhill's Honduran Selection, launched in 1998, and made in Danlí, consists of five sizes blended with filler leaf from the Dominican Republic, Mexico and Brazil, with binders from Mexico and Indonesian wrappers. This complex blend is designed to give a balanced medium smoke with a spicy finish. They are cigars very much for the experienced smoker seeking a fuller flavour. Dunhill's other two lines are made in the Dominican Republic and the Canary Islands (see pages 181 and 216).

PETRUS

Launched in 1990, this excellent brand, made in the La Flor de Copan factory, has succeeded in producing well-made, mild but interesting cigars, with pale wrappers grown from Connecticut seed in Ecuador, and binders and fillers from Honduras. There is a useful range of sensibly priced sizes. The limited edition Etiquette Rouge line (using filler leaf from Honduras, the Dominican Republic and Nicaragua) was launched in 1997 and offers a richer flavour.

Dunhill Lonsdale

Dunhill Tubed Corona

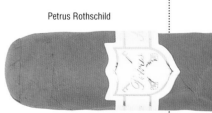

Petrus Rothschild

NICARAGUA
AND
COSTA RICA

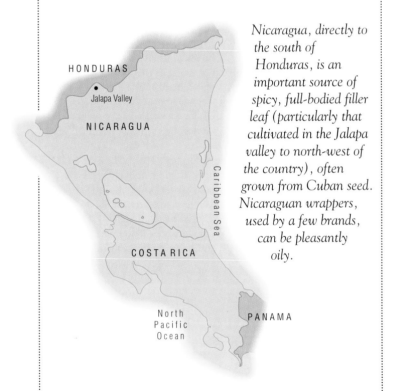

Nicaragua, directly to the south of Honduras, is an important source of spicy, full-bodied filler leaf (particularly that cultivated in the Jalapa valley to north-west of the country), often grown from Cuban seed. Nicaraguan wrappers, used by a few brands, can be pleasantly oily.

Joya de Nicaragua Petit Corona

Joya de Nicaragua Churchill

However, political upheavals and natural disasters have taken their toll of the nation's cigar industry. Nicaraguan cigars were highly rated in the 1970s, but the takeover by the left-wing Sandinista government in 1979 led to economic collapse (particularly after the suspension of American aid in 1981) and a civil war against the American-backed Contras. The Sandinistas relinquished power in 1990, but the war and economic situation continued to affect both tobacco production and cigar manufacture – not least because many tobacco plantations had been destroyed, and a number of the country's leading cigar producers had left Nicaragua.

As a result, cigars which appeared on the market during the early 1990s left much to be desired. Then, in 1998, just as the industry was finding its feet again, Hurricane Mitch struck, producing floods over large tracts of the country, including tobacco fields and factories. But things are gradually getting back to normal at the time of writing. Nicaraguan leaf is often found in the filler blends of Honduran or Dominican cigars.

Costa Rica, bordering southern Nicaragua, is starting to find a place in the cigar world as a provider of high-quality filler leaf, but is not yet a major manufacturer of cigars although, for instance, some C.A.O. cigars are produced there.

WHAT TO BUY —
NICARAGUAN
AND
COSTA RICAN
CIGARS

Joya de Nicaragua Elegante

JOYA DE NICARAGUA

THIS IS THE LEADING Nicaraguan brand, and once considered to be one of the best non-Cubans around. But the civil war and Nicaragua's economic problems had a serious effect on the quality of the cigars. Those produced in the early 1990s were made of leaf which hadn't been properly matured, with predictable consequences for both aroma and flavour. There were also construction problems. But things have improved considerably, and with good luck, these cigars might well regain their reputation. They come in a large range of sizes and offer a slightly peppery, mild to medium flavour.

PADRON

Padron Cigars, founded by José O. Padron in Miami,
has been producing handmade cigars using Nicaraguan
tobacco since 1964. The organization has companies
in both Nicaragua and Honduras (the former founded
in 1970, the latter in 1978) and is a stickler for quality
control.

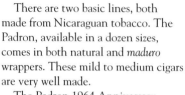

There are two basic lines, both
made from Nicaraguan tobacco. The
Padron, available in a dozen sizes,
comes in both natural and *maduro*
wrappers. These mild to medium cigars
are very well made.

The Padron 1964 Anniversary
series, launched in 1994, has a more
limited production. The leaf is aged at
least four years and, again, the cigars
come in both natural and *maduro*
wrappers. They are smooth, rich and
medium-bodied. Two new sizes,
Principe and Imperial, were recently
introduced, so that eight sizes are now
available.

The Padron Anniversary
Millennium was produced to celebrate
the year 2000. The cigar is 6 inches
(15 cm) long with a 52 ring gauge and
production was limited to 2,000 boxes
of 100 cigars each.

Padron Exclusivo

Padron 3000

OTHER
CIGAR-PRODUCING
COUNTRIES

MEXICO

DARK, PEPPERY MEXICAN leaf has been used for binders for some time, but now Mexican tobacco is also increasingly being used for wrappers (typically dark brown), and to add sweetness and richness to filler blends of cigars made elsewhere. But the country, which has an old cigar tradition (not to mention the fact that it was probably the first place where tobacco was cultivated), also produces a number of good handmades of its own: though none of them can be said to be in the first division of cigars. The best leaf comes from the San Andres Valley in southern Mexico. Some of it is grown from Sumatra seed, introduced by Dutch cigar manufacturers in the 1950s. Havana seed tobacco is grown in the Veracruz area further north.

Mexican cigars offer good value, and Mexico has also become a source of Havana cigars for Americans, and of contraband cigars smuggled into the United States. But many fakes are also on sale.

Te-Amo

Te-Amo No. 4

Perhaps the best-known Mexican brand, founded in the mid-1960s with a reputation for a punchy, some would say roughish, medium flavour and good construction. They come in a wide range of sizes, including a

number of figurados, and in a choice of light brown or *maduro* wrappers. The wrappers were rather coarse in the past, but quality has improved over the last few years, now that the brand is owned by the Consolidated Cigar Corporation. These cigars have their fans, particularly in the United States, not least for their low prices. All the tobacco used is Mexican.

Santa Clara

One of the best of Mexican cigars, made in San Andres with local wrappers. The filler blend is a mixture of sweetish San Andres leaf and fuller Havana seed tobacco from Veracruz. The cigars are well made and medium-flavoured, and come in a comprehensive range of sizes. The year 1830 found on the bands refers not to the date of the brand's origin, but a rough guess as to when the Ortiz family, which started the brand, first got involved in tobacco.

Santa Clara No. IV

Macanudo Portofino

JAMAICA

CIGARS HAVE BEEN made in Jamaica since the 19th century, originally for the British market, but current production consists of just a few important brands, all made by American companies, mostly with imported tobacco. Jamaican cigars have come to be known for their mild flavour.

Caribbean
Sea

JAMAICA

Kingston

Caribbean
Sea

MACANUDO

At the time of writing, Macanudo is the best-selling premium cigar brand in the United States. And not without some reason. The brand, originally founded by the Palicio family in Cuba as an offshoot of Punch, moved production to Jamaica during the Second World War so that they could come within the Sterling area, and continue to be sold to Britain. At the time, they had Cuban wrappers. The brand is also

Macanudo Vintage No. I

Macanudo's Duke of Devonshire.

made in the Dominican Republic – using the same blend – but the vast majority of Macanudos are still made in Jamaica by General Cigar. The word *macanudo*, though Spanish, is really only used in Argentina, and means 'fine and dandy', 'the best' or 'the ultimate.'

They are elegant and well made, and the smooth, mild flavour appeals to many beginners as well as to connoisseurs who like a mild daytime smoke, though some find them low on aroma. Wrappers are of Connecticut Shade leaf, binders from the San Andres area of Mexico, and the filler blend is a mixture of Jamaican, Mexican and Dominican tobacco.

There are more than 20 sizes of Macanudo to choose from, and, in some cases, a choice of wrappers as well: Café (Connecticut Shade), Jade (very mild and wrapped in double *claro*) and *maduro* (fuller, dressed with dark Mexican leaf). The cigars are usually individually wrapped in cellophane, with a couple of sizes (Hampton Court and Portofino) available in smart white tubes.

Macanudos as a whole are relatively expensive, and those with red bands and sold as Macanudo Vintage are even more costly, liked by connoisseurs for their fuller flavour.

The latest addition to the Macanudo range is the richer (but smooth) Macanudo Robust line, with six sizes currently available. Macanudo Robusts carry a distinctive 'R' logo and come in a dark green box. A pet project of General Cigar's Edgar Cullman, these very good cigars are made in the Dominican Republic with filler of Piloto Cubano, Havana seed binders (grown in Connecticut), and dark aged Connecticut Shade wrappers. They are distinctly different from other Macanudos.

ROYAL JAMAICA

Production of this brand returned to Jamaica in 1997, at a factory at May Pen, about an hour west of Kingston. The cigars had been made in Kingston until 1988, when Hurricane Gilbert ravaged both the factory and tobacco crops. Production was then moved to the Dominican Republic. Royal Jamaica is consistently

Royal Jamaica Park Lane

Royal Jamaica Double Corona

Royal Jamaica Pirate

among the best of mild cigar brands, with an abundant variety of shapes and sizes. The blend is predominantly Jamaican tobacco, with a Mexican binder and a silky Indonesian Java wrapper. A new size, Toro, (6 inches/15 cm x 50) was recently introduced. The fuller-bodied Maduro line combines Jamaican filler with a Cameroon binder and a dark Mexican wrapper – resulting in a richer taste with a hint of sweetness.

TEMPLE HALL

A brand dating from 1876, which was revived by General Cigar in the mid-1990s. The cigars are rather similar to Macanudo, but fuller-bodied. Leaves for the filler blend come from Jamaica, the Dominican Republic and Mexico; binders are Mexican, and wrappers for these superior cigars are Connecticut Shade, except in the case of the 450 (all the cigars are numbered rather than named) which has a dark wrapper from Mexico. There are seven sizes.

Temple Hall 550

Temple Hall 450

BRAZIL

B RAZIL HAS LONG had a cigar-manufacturing industry, and dark Brazilian leaf – flavourful, aromatic, sweet and a little peppery, though relatively mild – has been used by a number of European machine-made brands over the years. But now Brazilian filler leaves – the best grown in the Bahia area – are in demand for handmade cigars produced in the Dominican Republic and Honduras. Brazilian binders and dark brown wrappers (grown from Sumatra seed) are also used by some brands. Brazil's own best-known handmade brands are Suerdieck (mild to medium-flavoured) and the same manufacturer's Don Pepe (medium to full, with an earthy taste). But Brazilian cigars, though they have their adherents, haven't yet reached the front rank of fine smokes.

Suerdieck Brasilia

Don Pepe Double Corona

ECUADOR

Ecuador has no notable cigar industry to speak of, but high-quality wrapper leaf from the country (grown from Connecticut seed) is now being used on many brands made elsewhere. Unusually, the leaf isn't grown under shade, as heavy cloud cover limits the amount of direct sunlight received by the plants.

THE PHILIPPINES

The former Spanish colony of the Philippines is a significant centre of cigar making, and tobacco has long been an important export crop. But mild Philippines tobacco is really only used for locally-made cigars. They are not very widely exported, except to Spain. But one handmade Philippine brand which managed to acquire a following, and broader distribution, is called Calixto Lopez in the United States, and Carlos V elsewhere. The brand, made on Luzon – the largest island in the Philippines – dates from 1881, is well constructed, and mild to medium in flavour.

Don Pepe Churchill

Don Pepe Robusto

Tobacco field, Java.

INDONESIA

Just as the Spanish were responsible for the tobacco and cigar industries of the Philippines, the former Dutch colony of Indonesia (the islands of Sumatra and Java in particular) have become important producers of sought-after wrapper leaf (particularly Jember) for handmades, as well as a major source of leaf for mass-market cigars machine-made in The Netherlands, Germany and Switzerland. Tobacco cultivation dates back to the 18th century. Shade-grown tobacco, known as TBN (some of it a hybrid of local and Connecticut strains) is also grown on the island of Java. Some filler and binder leaf is also used for handmades from the Dominican Republic and Honduras. Indonesian cigar tobacco is typically medium bodied and peppery.

CAMEROON

Cameroon in West Africa has been an important source of high-quality wrapper leaf for some years. At their best, Cameroon wrappers – grown from Sumatra seed – are medium to dark brown and rich. They are used to dress a number of leading handmade brands.

THE UNITED STATES

The United States is the world's biggest premium cigar market, arguably the most important country after Spain and Cuba in the historical development of cigars and cigar smoking – and the undisputed leader of the 1990s cigar boom.

There was once a flourishing handmade cigar industry in the United States, centred in Florida with its large émigré Cuban population, particularly in the Tampa area. But today, the United States itself produces few premium cigars of note, with a shift of production by major manufacturers (such as General Cigar and the

Consolidated Cigar Corporation), as well as smaller companies, to the Caribbean and Central America – to take advantage of the local tobacco supply and low labour costs.

The vast majority of cigars produced in the United States today are mass-market machine-mades.

AMERICAN WRAPPERS

The United States produces some of the world's best and most expensive wrapper tobacco, called Connecticut Shade. It is grown from the Hazelwood strain of Cuban seed on the sandy loam of the Connecticut river valley under 10-foot-high tents. The growing cycle begins in March, with harvesting in August. The curing process is helped by heat created from below by gas burners. The cost of cultivating the leaves in this way adds substantially to the price of the many famous brands they wrap. The wrappers are smooth and silky, and tend to be light brown to mid-brown in colour. They are normally used to wrap mild- and medium-flavoured cigars.

A different type of tobacco, Connecticut broadleaf, is also used for wrappers. It is grown in the sun, and by the time it is matured, is very dark, slightly coarse, and used for cigars sold as *maduro*.

SPAIN

The nation which developed the cigar as we know it is the world's biggest importer of Havana cigars, as well as still producing locally handmade brands (cigar smoking is a big feature of bull fights), none

Roller in cigar factory, La Palma, Tenerife.

Dunhill Panatela

Dunhill Corona Extra

of them of any importance elsewhere. However, the Spanish tobacco monopoly, Tabacalera, is an important force in the cigar world. And the Canary Islands, the Spanish outpost off the Atlantic coast of North Africa, are an important centre of premium cigar manufacture, though not quite so much as in the 1960s and 1970s. It was where a number of leading Cuban cigar makers restarted production after Castro's revolution. Brands made there included Don Diego, Don Miguel and Montecruz (founded by the Menendez family, once owners of Montecristo), but production of these brands, and others, eventually moved to the Dominican Republic.

Perhaps the best-known cigars currently being made in the Canary Islands are those from Dunhill (which also has lines made in the Dominican Republic and Honduras). The range is small, numbering just five sizes. Distinguished by their brown and gold bands, these cigars offer a mild to medium flavour with a touch of sweetness. They are well constructed, but offer a somewhat less polished smoke than other Dunhills. They are only available in the United States.

FRANCE

This was one of the first European countries outside Spain to take up cigar manufacture – with production starting at Morlaix, in Brittany, as early as 1740. But although cigar culture flourishes in France, and despite the fact that the French tobacco monopoly, Seita, has struck a number of important deals with the Cubans over the years, and is an important player in the world of smoking, the great majority of cigars produced in France are undistinguished mass-market machine-mades.

THE U.K., NETHERLANDS, GERMANY, SWITZERLAND AND ITALY

One of the world's most trustworthy and important markets for Havana cigars: British importers have had a great influence on the development of Havana brands over the years. But the few British cigar brands on the market are machine-made for the mass market, and poor even when compared to their Continental equivalents from The Netherlands, Germany and Switzerland. These nations, The Netherlands in particular, have a long tradition of machine-made cigar manufacture – usually using tobacco from Sumatra, Brazil, and sometimes Cuba. The Dutch Agio company, indeed, recently launched the handmade Balmoral brand (made in the Dominican Republic). If you want to smoke a cheap machine-made cigar, buy a brand made in these countries.

Italy is known only for its strong, and rather bitter Toscani cigars, which are very much an acquired taste. There are tobacco fields in Tuscany.

Machine-made Agios,
above and below.

CIGAR
PEOPLE

A
WHO'S WHO
OF CIGAR
SMOKERS

ADAMS, JOHN QUINCY
SIXTH PRESIDENT of the United States, who was a cigar lover, as were his successors James Madison, Andrew Jackson (whose wife Rachel joined him), Zachary Taylor (whose son-in-law, Jefferson Davis, President of the Confederacy, also smoked), William McKinley, W.H. Taft, Warren Harding, Calvin Coolidge and Herbert Hoover.

BARTHÉLMY, AUGUSTE
French 19th-century poet who, in 1849, wrote a *Manual on the Art of Smoking* in 5,000 Alexandrine verses. These included:

> *For the man who is not a hapless layman, 'neath the firmament nothing surpasses the Havana cigar.*
> *The sun that browns it swells with pride.*

and:

> *It is necessary to know how to smoke so that one knows how to choose.*
> *The true smoker abstains from imitating Vesuvius.*
> *He demonstrates the requirement that during three-quarters of an hour*
> *A cigar rests in his hand without going out.*

BEAVERBROOK, LORD
The Canadian-born newspaper magnate, and British politician (wartime minister of aircraft production, and owner of *The Daily Express*), shared a love of Havana cigars with his friends Winston Churchill and Somerset Maugham.

BERLE, MILTON

The veteran comedian and former vaudevillian was long a smoker of fine cigars.

BISMARCK, OTTO VON

The 19th-century 'Iron Chancellor' of Germany was a fond smoker of cigars. Once, riding unaccompanied down the Bois de Boulogne in Paris after the French surrender following the Franco-Prussian war of 1870, Bismarck sensed hostility from those around him, but soon diffused a potentially dangerous situation by asking a passer-by for a light for his cigar.

BOCK, GUSTAVE

The Dutchman credited with inventing the cigar band in the 19th century. He was one of the first Europeans to own a Cuban tobacco plantation, and wrote *The Art of Smoking the Cigar*.

BONAPARTE, NAPOLEON

Emperor of France, of whom it was said, 'One could always tell where the French Emperor had stopped a few moments by the quantity of tobacco strewn on the floor.' He was also indirectly responsible for the spread of cigar smoking in Britain and France – a habit learned in Spain and brought back by officers who had served in the Peninsular War. His nephew, Napoleon III, when asked to ban smoking, remarked: "This vice brings in a hundred million a year in taxes. I shall certainly ban it at once – as soon as you can name a virtue that raises as much money."

BULWER-LYTTON, EDWARD

The Victorian poet, novelist and politician (later Lord Lytton) wrote, in 1845: 'A good cigar is as great a comfort to a man as a good cry to a woman.'

BURNS, GEORGE

The great American comic, who died in 1996, aged over 100, was rarely seen without a cigar in his mouth. He made his Oscar-winning screen comeback (aged 79) in *The Sunshine Boys*, after an absence of 35 years. His earlier performances were usually alongside his late wife Gracie Allen. When asked what his doctor thought of his cigar smoking, he replied: "I don't know, my doctor's dead." He was paid to promote the cheap American El Producto brand, but justified it by saying that more expensive cigars went out too often to be useable in his stage act.

BYRON, LORD
The famed British poet, rake and advocate of Greek nationalism. His ode *Sublime Tobacco*, in *The Island*, ends with the lines:

> *Yet thy true lovers more adore by far*
> *Thy naked beauties - Give me a cigar!*

A Cuban brand was once named after him.

CAINE, SIR MICHAEL
The British film star has been a fond handmade cigar smoker ever since he found fame in the 1960s with the films *Zulu* and *Alfie*. He buys his cigars in London, in a box of 50 containing a selection of ten each of Montecristo sizes 1-5. He has been known to refer to it as "a box of allsorts." Born Maurice Micklewhite, he was once a fish porter, before he turned to acting.

CARUSO, ENRICO
The great opera singer, who died aged only 48 in 1921, had a clause in his contracts demanding 'the right to smoke on any part of the stage from the moment the curtain rises.'

CASANOVA, GIACOMO
The famous 18th-century Venetian seducer, who mentions the cigar in his autobiography, *History of My Life*, one of the first literary references.

CASTRO, FIDEL
The Cuban communist leader who overthrew General Fulgencio Batista in 1959 was a keen cigar smoker (one CIA plot to get rid of him involved tampering with his cigars). But he stopped smoking some years ago to try to discourage his fellow countrymen from smoking so much – around 250 million cigars a year. When he was held prisoner on the island of Pines, in 1955, his followers sent him messages rolled into cigars.

CHAPLIN, CHARLIE
Frequently seen with a cigar in his mouth in his films. He died in 1977, not long after being awarded a knighthood. His daughter, Geraldine, has also been known to smoke panatela cigars.

CHE GUEVARA, ERNESTO
The Argentine-born revolutionary, and left-wing cult hero, who became Cuban minister of industry, and later met his end (in 1967) in Bolivia. A doctor by training, he once wrote: 'An habitual and

---

extremely important complement in the life of a guerilla is smoking ... for the smoke that he can expel in moments of relaxation is a great companion to the lonely soldier.'

CHURCHILL, SIR WINSTON

The great British war leader is one of the most famous and dedicated cigar smokers in history. He favoured big cigars (often double coronas) with dark wrappers, which he would usually only smoke halfway through. He is thought to have smoked more than 200,000 cigars during his long life. Many of them were supplied to him free by companies such as Jamaica Tobacco Co, and Hoyo de Monterrey, then owned by Palicio. But Churchill had to fight regularly with British Customs and Excise to keep the cigars given to him without paying duty on them. A later British Prime Minister, Harold Wilson, who smoked a pipe in public, but cigars in private, had a similar problem in the 1960s when Fidel Castro sent him two 10lb boxes of cigars.

Churchill first encountered Havanas when he went to Cuba in 1895 during the Spanish-American war, and he later bought his supplies from Robert Lewis, the great London cigar merchant, as well as from Dunhill. The shop's records show that his first order was placed in 1900, and the last a month before he died in 1965. He once said: "I always carry Cuba in my mouth." He is one of the few people to have had a cigar size named after him, originally by Romeo Y Julieta, but later also by many other brands. The standard Churchill size is 7 inches x 47 ring gauge, but there are many somewhat different sizes of cigar also bearing the name.

During the Blitz, after a German bomb hit the Dunhill shop, a flustered manager telephoned him at 2am in the morning with the message, "Your cigars are safe, sir."

When Field Marshal Montgomery once said to him: "I do not drink. I do not smoke. I sleep a great deal. That is why I am 100 per cent fit, " Churchill riposted: "I drink a great deal. I sleep little, and I smoke cigar after cigar. That is why I am 200 per cent fit."

On a similar note, hosting a lunch for the King of Saudi Arabia (Ibn Saud), Churchill asked an

Hoyo de Monterrey Double Corona

interpreter to say, "that if it was the religion of His Majesty to deprive himself of smoking and alcohol, I must point out that my rule of life prescribed as an absolutely sacred rite is the smoking of cigars and also the drinking of alcohol before, after, and if need be during all meals and in the intervals between them."

Churchill's daughter, Lady Soames, widow of the former British ambassador and cabinet minister, Christopher Soames, is a dedicated cigar smoker, a habit she inherited from her father. In his controversial diaries, Lord Wyatt wrote: 'Mary smoked a cigar after dinner. Quite a big one. She said Papa didn't smoke as many cigars as people thought.' In fact, it was claimed in a book published in the late 1990s that in the last 15 years of his life, Churchill only really wielded a cigar (and a brandy if necessary) for the cameras.

CIFUENTES
This great Cuban cigar-making family owned the Partagas factory from 1920, and other brands such as Ramon Allones.

CLAY, HENRY
The 19th-century American Senator, who had financial interests in Cuba, and a brand named after him.

CLINTON, WILLIAM JEFFERSON
It is a matter of speculation whether Bill Clinton, 42nd President of the United States, still smokes cigars, though we know he couldn't possibly inhale. His wife banned smoking at the White House, but at least one cigar – not smoked as far as is known – became famous in his relationship with White House intern Monica Lewinsky.

COBURN, JAMES
The star of such films as *The Great Escape*, *Major Dundee*, and *Cross of Iron* is one of Hollywood's most knowledgeable cigar smokers. The Saint Luis Rey brand is one of his favourites.

Saint Luis Rey Serie 'A'.

COLETTE, SIDONIE GABRIELLE

The French novelist, who died in Paris in 1954, once observed: "When a wife can purchase her husband the right cigars, their relationship is blessed." In Gigi, the character Aunt Alice says: "Let me think how I will teach you to choose cigars... when a woman knows a man's preferences, cigars included, and when a man knows what pleases a woman, they are well armed for life together."

COLTRANE, ROBBIE

Born Robin McMillan, the portly Scottish TV star and actor in the James Bond films *Goldeneye* and *The World is Not Enough*, among a number of other feature films, is a keen cigar smoker. He started on giving up cigarettes. He likes Hoyo de Monterrey Epicure No. 2s (a robusto size, like the man himself) and, sometimes, Montecristo No. 4.

Hoyo de Monterrey Cabinet Epicure No. 2.

CONRAN, SIR TERENCE

British businessman, restaurateur and design guru, founder of the Habitat furnishing chain, and of some of London's best-known restaurants. His favourite smoke is El Rey del Mundo. One of his sons, Tom, also a restaurant owner, albeit on a smaller scale, is also a fond cigar smoker.

COPPOLA, FRANCIS FORD

The director of such memorable films as *Apocalypse Now*, *The Godfather*, *The Cotton Club* and Bram Stoker's *Dracula*, is a regular cigar smoker, a habit he inherited from his father Carmine (who liked Italian cigars such as Toscani). He owns a gold and silver cigar cutter which once belonged to the studio boss Jack Warner. Warner taught him how to light a cigar properly. He is also a wine producer, with vineyards in California's Napa Valley.

CRUISE, TOM

The film star, whose films include *Top Gun* and *Eyes Wide Shut*, favours Cohiba. A few years ago, he asked the London importers Hunters & Frankau to find him 1,000 Cohiba Robustos.

DAVIDOFF, ZINO

Russian-born, and one of the greatest names in the cigar world. His father had a tobacco shop in Kiev, and Davidoff followed him into the business when the family moved to Switzerland in 1912. He spent two years in Cuba in his youth, learning about all aspects of tobacco cultivation and cigar making. In 1945, he developed his Château series along with the Hoyo de Monterrey factory, and in 1969, had a Havana brand, with its distinctive white and gold band, named after him.

Davidoff – his business owned by a Swiss corporation by then – fell out with the Cubans in the 1980s, and cigars bearing his name now come from the Dominican Republic, where they have been made since 1990. But Cuban Davidoffs now fetch very high prices. In 1983, Davidoff introduced the Honduras-made Zino brand to the United States.

Zino Connoisseur 100

Davidoff has become perhaps the world's greatest cigar merchant. The Davidoff shops around the world (the main one is in Geneva, the others are mostly franchised) are temples to smoking, selling many accessories as well as cigars. Davidoff wrote two books on cigars and cigar smoking (the last being *The Connoisseur's Book of the Cigar*), both originally published in French.

DEVITO, DANNY

The actor and director smokes Cohiba Corona Especials and Robustos – bought from the Davidoff shop in London.

DON JUAN

The legendary Spanish seducer was a keen smoker of Sevillas.

DUFY, RAOUL

The French painter, who died in 1953, and was famous for his bold use of colour, and his paintings depicting bathers, boats and racing.

He was a confirmed cigar smoker, who often exchanged his pictures for cigars.

DUNHILL, ALFRED

Founder of the famous cigar shops in London and New York, at the beginning of the 20th century. He is the author of *The Gentle Art of Smoking*.

The old English company of Alfred Dunhill can claim a long association with fine cigars. It was to Dunhill that the Menendez y Garcia company first took their infant Montecristo brand in 1935; the firm also housed brands such as Don Candido and Don Alfredo. The 1980s saw the brief creation of Dunhill's own brand of Havanas, sporting a red band bearing the company's elongated 'd' logo on cigars bearing names such as Cabinetta, Malecon and Mojito. Cuban production stopped in 1989. You might still find some Cuban Dunhills lurking around – at very high prices. The firm has branched out into luggage, clothing, and all manner of accessories, but the name is still synonymous with smoking. Dunhill handmade cigars now come from the Dominican Republic, Honduras and the Canary Islands.

EDWARD VII, KING OF ENGLAND

As Prince of Wales (there is a Romeo Y Julieta named after him) he did much, as a leader of fashion, to make cigar smoking chic. He preferred double coronas, bearing his personal band featuring the Prince of Wales' emblem – three white ostrich plumes. His mother, Queen Victoria, hated smoking, and banned it from her presence. When he became King, he was able to say to his Court: "Gentlemen, you may smoke." The American mass-market machine-made brand, King Edward, is named after him.

Today's British royal family has no keen cigar smokers, although Prince Philip and Lord Snowdon (the photographer, and former husband of Princess Margaret) have both displayed a fondness for cigars in the past; and there is a Macanudo named after Prince Philip. Princess Margaret's furniture-designer son, Lord Linley, has designed a number of elaborate humidors, based on farmhouse buildings.

Macanudo Prince Philip

FAROUK I, KING OF EGYPT

The ill-fated playboy king, who died in exile in Rome in 1965, was a devoted smoker of big cigars, particularly double coronas. He used to buy a minimum of 5,000 cigars a time. He was once supposed to have ordered 40,000 Hoyo de Monterrey double coronas from the Davidoff shop in Geneva. The aptly named Visible Immenso cigar, measuring 18 inches x 47 ring gauge, was specially made for him.

Montecristos.

FINNEY, ALBERT

The British actor – as fine on stage as he is on the big screen – graduated from working class hero parts on stage and in films such as *Saturday Night and Sunday Morning* to more prosperous characters like Hercule Poirot in *Murder on the Orient Express*, and a political boss in *Miller's Crossing*, in which he takes his time to smoke a cigar. His true tastes are shown by his fondness for horse racing (his father was a bookie, but Finney actually owns racehorses) and Montecristo No. 1s.

FOCH, MARSHAL FERDINAND

The French hero of The First World War, appointed Chief of Staff of the French army in 1917, and Commander in Chief of the Allied armies the following year. He was a master strategist and tactician who found that cigars helped him to concentrate, particularly when he had a big military decision to make.

FREUD, SIGMUND

The Viennese founder of psychoanalysis was a habitual cigar smoker from the age of 24. Shortly before his death, he said: "I owe to the cigar a great intensification of my capacity to work and a facilitation of my self-control". Though

just what followers of his theories make of the symbolism of his cigar smoking, or the unconscious urge it represented, is anybody's guess.

FROST, SIR DAVID
The transatlantic TV host and interviewer has been a dedicated cigar smoker ever since he first came to fame with the British TV show *That Was the Week That Was* in the 1960s. He used to favour big Cuban-made Davidoffs.

GLENN, JOHN
The highly decorated Second World War marine corps flyer and test pilot became the first man to orbit the Earth in the space capsule Friendship 7 in 1962. After retiring from the space programme, Colonel Glenn became a businessman and Democratic senator. In 1984, he stood unsuccessfully as a presidential candidate.

According to Zino Davidoff, when he returned from space, he was given his own weight in Havanas, even though the United States embargo on Cuba was already in force. The first cigar in space went up with the Russian Soyuz-38 craft in 1980. It was a specially made Cuban corona, $5^3/_4$ inches x 42 ring gauge. The filler leaf came from San Juan y Martínez and San Luis in the Vuelta Abajo, the binder from Santa Damiana, also in Vuelta Abajo, and the wrapper from Partido, in Havana province. The band was in the Cuban national colours of blue, white and red, with a white star in the centre.

Montecristo A

GRADE, LORD
Lew Grade, the British TV tycoon and film producer, who started life as a Charleston dancer, and died aged 91, was rarely seen without a Montecristo A in his mouth. He smoked six a day. Before the launch of the Montecristo A, he used to smoke specially imported Amorvana Giants from Jamaica. His nephew, Michael, former head of the British Channel 4 TV station, continues the family cigar tradition.

GRANT, ULYSSES S.
The American Civil War general and eventual 18th President of the United States used to smoke ten cigars a day, but this number went up to as many as 20 to 25 cigars, particularly after he received thousands as gifts from admirers. His campaign song, when he ran for the Presidency, was *A-Smokin' His Cigar*.

GULBENKIAN, NUBAR
The colourful Armenian oil magnate (his father was the original 'Mr Five Percent'), favoured Partagas cigars, which he continued to smoke after the Cuban revolution, buying them in Prague, and paying through a Soviet bank. He once said: "Even if the devil were to take possession of the Vuelta, I would continue to smoke Havana cigars."

When staying at the Ritz in London, he used to travel around in a specially converted, chauffeur-driven black London taxicab with basket-work doors. He was famous for his remark: "They tell me it turns on a sixpence, whatever that is."

Partagas Shorts

HEMINGWAY, ERNEST
The American novelist, and long-time resident of Cuba, where his house is still preserved as a museum, was as keen on cigars as he was on bullfights, sea-fishing and big game hunting. A number of his novels and short stories use Cuban locations.

HITCHCOCK, SIR ALFRED
The great British film director, who died in 1980, aged 81, directed the first successful British 'talkie', *Blackmail*, as well as his later legendary suspense dramas. He was a keen cigar smoker both on the set and off. A number of his films have scenes involving cigars.

HOOD, THOMAS
In 1840, the British poet wrote *The Cigar*:

> *Some sigh for this and that;*
> *My wishes don't go far;*
> *The world may wag at will,*
> *So I have my cigar.*

HUGO, VICTOR
The French writer once called tobacco 'the plant that converts thoughts into dreams.' His works were amongst the most popular to be read to cigar rollers in Havana factories during the 19th and early 20th centuries.

JONES, TOM
The Welsh ballad singer and former miner is a regular smoker of handmade cigars. A short man, he nonetheless prefers the very long Montecristo A.

KENNEDY, JOHN F.
Although President Kennedy imposed the trade embargo on Cuba as a result of the 1962 Soviet weapons crisis, it wasn't until he had secured an adequate supply of cigars for himself. One evening, in February 1962, some months after the Bay of Pigs incident, Kennedy summoned his Press Secretary, and fellow cigar lover, Pierre Salinger, and asked him to find 1,000 Petit Upmanns by the following morning. At 8am the next day, an anxious Kennedy called him in again, and after being told that Salinger had managed to find as many as 1,200 cigars, immediately took out a pen and signed the decree banning all Cuban products from the United States.

A few months later Salinger (whose own favourite is Partagas Lusitania) found himself in Moscow for talks with Nikita Khrushchev. The Soviet leader, who didn't like cigars, gave Salinger a case of 250 Havanas. Knowing he would be breaking the embargo, Salinger decided he would, nonetheless, take them back to the United States, taking advantage of his diplomatic passport. When he reported back to Kennedy, with whom he had intended to share the cigars, the President, fearful of a scandal, immediately ordered him to declare them to U.S. Customs. Salinger duly did so but, to this day, suspects that though they may indeed have been destroyed, it was almost certainly one by one.

KIPLING, RUDYARD
The Nobel Prize-winning poet, author of *Gunga Din*, and other works celebrating the British Empire, was a cigar lover who (in *The*

Betrothed) came out with the line, now notorious, 'A woman is only a woman, but a good cigar is a smoke.' But the words have been widely misunderstood, when taken out of context. The poem is in fact satirical, about choosing between a woman, Maggie, and smoking, and was inspired by a breach of promise case brought in 1885:

> *Open the old cigar box, get me a Cuba stout,*
> *For things are running crossways, and Maggie and I are out.*
>
> *We quarrelled about Havanas – we fought o'er a good cheroot,*
> *And I know she is exacting, and she says I am a brute…*
>
> *…There's peace in a Larranaga, there's calm in a Henry Clay.*
> *But the best cigar in an hour is finished and thrown away –*
>
> *…Open the old cigar-box – let me consider a while.*
> *Here is a mild Manila – there is a wifely smile…*
>
> *Which is the better portion – bondage bought with a ring,*
> *Or a harem of dusky beauties, fifty tied in a string?…*
>
> *…A million surplus Maggies are willing to bear the yoke;*
> *And a woman is only a woman, but a good cigar is a Smoke.*
>
> *Light me another Cuba – I hold to my first-sworn vows.*
> *If Maggie will have no rival, I will have no Maggie for Spouse!*

LA ROCHEFOUCAULD, DUC DE

The 18th-century French diplomat (descendant of La Rochefoucauld, author of the famous *Maxims*), who was sent to liaise with the American revolutionary government in 1794, wrote of his voyage: 'The cigar is a great resource. It is necessary to have travelled for a long time on a ship to understand that at least the cigar affords you the pleasure of smoking. It raises your spirits. Are you troubled by something? The cigar will dissolve it. Are you harassed by unpleasant thoughts? Smoking a cigar puts one in a frame of mind to dispense with these…If you are obsessed by sad thoughts, a cigar will take your mind off them… Sometimes they die out, and happy are those who do not need to relight too quickly…"

LENIN, VLADIMIR ILYICH

The Russian revolutionary and Soviet leader used to buy cigars from Henri Davidoff's shop in Geneva. Zino Davidoff, his son, recorded that Vladimir Ulyanov, as he was known at the time, never paid his bill.

LISZT, FRANZ

The composer was an inveterate smoker who always carried a large box of cigars with him. He once said: "A good Cuban cigar closes the door to the vulgarities of the world."

LONSDALE, LORD

The British aristocrat and great cigar lover was one of the few people to give his name to a cigar size, created for him. It is now one of the most popular sizes available (usually 6 inches x 42 ring gauge). The Rafael Gonzalez brand used to carry his portrait on the inside of the box lid.

Rafael Gonzalez Lonsdale

MALLARME, STEPHANE

The French 19th-century poet once wrote: 'What voluptuousness when I lunched with my father... After finishing the meal he produced boxes of sparkling cigars: Valle, Clay, Upmann. I opened these boxes which evoked visions of dancing girls, and I removed the bands, because that is what is to be done...'

MARSHALL, THOMAS

United States vice-president under Woodrow Wilson, famous for the observation, made around 1920 to John Crockett, "What this country needs is a really good five-cent cigar." To which the comic Will Rogers later riposted: "Our country has plenty of good five-cent cigars, but the trouble is they charge 15 cents for them."

MARTÍ, JOSÉ

The Cuban revolutionary who led the revolt against Spain in 1895. His campaign was largely funded by exiled Cuban tobacco workers, and given dynamism by the increasingly politicized Cuban industrial working class, led by the cigar workers. News of his landing was sent, concealed in a cigar, to his supporters from Key West. One of the main Havana factories (formerly H. Upmann) is named after him. He once wrote of tobacco that it was the 'comfort of the pensive, delight of the daydreamer...' The earlier South American revolutionary, Benito Juarez, was also a cigar smoker.

MARX, GROUCHO

A dedicated cigar smoker, as a look at any of the Marx Brothers' films will testify. If ever a comedian had a trademark prop, it was Groucho and his cigar – although he rarely, if ever, smoked it on screen. Once, when his wife asked him to give up cigars, he said: "No, but we can remain good friends." On another occasion, a woman told him she had 22 children because she loved her husband. He replied: "I like my cigar, too. But I take it out of my mouth once in a while." He liked his cigars strong. A particular favourite was the Dunhill 410.

MARX, KARL

The political thinker led a ramshackle, impecunious and drunken life in London. And he was very fond of cigars. One day, in Holborn, he saw a tobacconist's window advertising (rather bad) cigars with the slogan: 'The more you smoke, the more you save.' He demonstrated his understanding of economics by telling his friends that he would save one shilling and sixpence per box if he bought them, and that if he smoked enough of them, he might one day be able to live on his 'savings'. But, as his recent biographer Francis Wheen wrote: 'The theory was tested with such lung-rasping commitment that eventually the family doctor had to intervene, ordering the wheezing patient to find some other way of enriching himself.'

MAUGHAM, SOMERSET

The British author of *Liza of Lambeth*, *The Moon and Sixpence* and *Of Human Bondage*, once the richest writer in the world, had a tortured life, well documented since his death. In his autobiography, *Summing Up*, he wrote: 'A good cigar is one of the best pleasures that I know. At the time when I was young and very poor, I only smoked cigars which were offered to me. I promised myself that if I ever had some money that I would savour a cigar each day after lunch and after dinner. This is the only resolution of my youth that I have kept, and the only realized ambition which has not brought disillusion. I like a mild cigar, of delicate aroma and medium length. If the cigar is too small, you cannot enjoy the smoke. If too fat, the smoke overwhelms you. The best cigar is one that you can roll without effort, that is wrapped in a leaf that does not dissolve in the mouth, and which keeps its aroma to the end.' He was, incidentally, a qualified doctor.

MENCKEN, HENRY LOUIS

The Baltimore-born American journalist and critic was the son of a cigar factory owner, August Mencken. He actually worked in his father's factory as a youngster, before setting himself on the path to becoming one of America's most celebrated commentators. He hated the cigar business, but loved cigars (having even rolled them). He ordered 300 cigars a month, but often couldn't smoke them fully thanks to bouts of hay fever. When a group of women called for cigars to be banned on Baltimore's trams, he wrote: 'Women, in general, are not nearly so delicate as romance makes them. A woman who can stand half an hour of the Lexington Fish Market is well able to face a few blasts of tobacco smoke.' He also said: "Not one in 10,000 [women] can tell the difference between good tobacco and bad."

MENENDEZ

One of the great Cuban cigar families, who owned H. Upmann and Montecristo, with the Garcias. The family left Cuba after the revolution to make Montecruz cigars in the Canary Islands. Later, Benjamin Menendez oversaw the production of General Cigar's brands (including Partagas, Temple Hall and Macanudo) made in Jamaica and the Dominican Republic.

MURRAY, SIR CHARLES

In his book *Visit to Cuba* (1836), Murray wrote of cigars: 'Some of the best I have smoked in my life were some cigars given me by an English neighbour here in Havana, cigars which they had sent to Liverpool and which were returned because of their dark colour and ugly appearance. The double trip across the Atlantic cured them sufficiently so that they were the most delicious cigars that even a meditative philosopher could have dreamed.' And that, when sea air is normally thought to be extremely deleterious to the quality of cigars.

MUSSET, ALFRED DE

The 19th-century French poet, novelist and playwright (perhaps best known for *Lorenzaccio*) was a dedicated cigar smoker. He called the cigar 'the best way of killing time.' He also wrote: 'Any cigar smoker is a friend, because I know what he feels.

NETANYAHU, BENJAMIN

When still in office, the cigar-loving Israeli Prime Minister was eventually forced to pay for his own cigars, after it was revealed that his smokes (which he generously offered to guests and senior staff) were costing the taxpayer the equivalent of £2,000 sterling or about US$3,200 a month.

Temple Hall 700

ONASSIS, ARISTOTLE
The enormously wealthy Greek shipping millionaire loved cigars almost as much as did his friend Winston Churchill – and John Kennedy, whose widow he married. His father was a tobacco merchant and Onassis himself made his first million as a tobacco importer. His yacht *Christina* had a humidor on board. His shipping rival, Stavros Niarchos, favoured Partagas.

PALICIO

The family which owned Hoyo de Monterrey and Punch before the Cuban Revolution. The trademarks passed to Villazon, which now make cigars under these brand names in Honduras. But the Punch brand is most closely associated with Fernando Palicio, its last private owner, who also owned the Belinda brand. He was important for popularizing the half corona size (Petit Punch), particularly in Britain.

PILSUDSKI, JOZEF
Polish First World War military leader, and later head of state. He said of smoking: "I shall never be separated from the friend who helped me spend the most enjoyable moments of my life."

RAINIER, PRINCE OF MONACO
Always a keen cigar connoisseur, he is fond of Rafael Gonzalez Lonsdales, and was a fan of the Cuban Davidoff Château Margaux.

RAVEL, MAURICE
The French late 19th and early 20th-century composer of *Bolero* was a serious Havana smoker, who said smoking helped him to compose his orchestral works and those for piano. Fellow cigar lover, Colette, was the librettist for his best-known opera, *The Child and the Enchantment*.

ROBINSON, EDWARD G.
The great Hollywood movie star was as much a cigar smoker off screen as he was on. He was given the title 'Mister Cigar' by American importers in 1949 for his help in publicizing cigar smoking on the screen.

ROTHSCHILD

The French branch of the famous banking family have long been cigar connoisseurs. They allowed the name of some of their most celebrated wines to be used by Zino Davidoff for his Château series of cigars. Later, when the Zino Mouton Cadet series was launched in the 1980s, Baroness Phillipine de Rothschild accompanied Davidoff on a promotional tour of the United States. Rothschild is the name sometimes given to the robusto size in non-Cuban markets.

Zino Mouton Cadet No. 1

Zino Mouton Cadet No. 2

Zino Mouton Cadet No. 3

RUBINSTEIN, ARTUR

The Polish-born pianist, eventually a U.S. citizen, who died in 1982 loved cigars. He even owned a plantation in the Vuelta Abajo region of Cuba before the revolution and used personalized bands with his face on them. He had the foresight to secure enough Havanas for the rest of his life before the revolution, stored at the Dunhill shop in New York. He favoured Romeo Y Julieta.

SAND, GEORGE

The female French 19th-century novelist (she was christened Amandine-Aurore Lucille Dupin), and Chopin's longstanding lover, smoked cigars and once wrote: 'Cigars calm pain and people loneliness with a thousand gracious images.'

SAVILE, SIR JIMMY

British disc jockey, showbusiness personality and untiring charity worker, once a miner, is devoted to full-flavoured Bolivar coronas extra cigars which he buys in the Dunhill shop in London. His friend, Prince Charles, a non-smoker, used to give him the Cohibas he received as gifts from Fidel Castro.

SCHWARZENEGGER, ARNOLD

One of the biggest box office names in movies today, as well as a shrewd businessman, Austrian-born Schwarzenegger is now married to TV presenter Maria Shriver, a member of the Kennedy family. The former body-builder buys his favourite Cohiba Esplendidos in London.

SCOTT, RIDLEY

The British film director, famed for his visual flair (he originally trained as a designer) in films such as *Blade Runner*, *Alien* and *Thelma and Louise*, is a Cohiba smoker. Appropriate for the man who made *1492*, the epic film (starring Gérard Depardieu) about Columbus's momentous voyage.

SIBELIUS, JEAN

The Finnish composer, who died aged 92 in 1957, was a cigar lover, who once wrote in thanks for a gift of Cuban cigars sent on his 83rd birthday: 'Since one of my uncles lived and died in Cuba, I have always been greatly interested in your admirable country. Moreover, I have smoked Havana cigars all my life and, of course, they have always been highly meaningful for me.'

SINATRA, FRANK

'Ol Blue Eyes', when he smoked, liked Lonsdales, particularly the Saint Luis Rey, and the Montecristo No 1.

STENDHAL

French early 19th-century novelist (his real name was Henri Beyle), and author of *The Red and the Black*, often mentioned cigars in his work. He lived in Italy from 1814-1821, and smoked Italian Toscani cigars. 'On a cold morning in winter, a Toscani cigar fortifies the soul,' he wrote.

THACKERAY, WILLIAM MAKEPEACE -

The 19th-century English novelist used to kick-off his working day with a cigar, and cigars feature in works such as *Vanity Fair*. In *Sketches and Travels in London* he wrote: 'Honest men, with pipes and cigars in their mouths, have great physical advantages in conversation...the cigar harmonizes the society, and soothes at once the speaker and the subject whereon he converses...I vow and believe that the cigar has been one of the greatest creature comforts of my life – a kind companion, a gentle stimulant, an amiable anodyne, a cementer of friendship.'

TWAIN, MARK

The great American humorist and author of *The Adventures of Tom Sawyer* and *The Adventures of Huckleberry Finn*, was well-known for cigar smoking: he could get through around 300 cheap cigars a month, many more if writing a book. Brought up on the Mississippi, he started smoking at the age of eight. After marrying, he lived in Hartford, Connecticut from 1867 to 1890, a leading centre of cigar production. He once wrote: 'If cigar smoking is not permitted in Heaven, I won't go.'

On trying to cut down his smoking, he wrote: 'I pledged myself to smoke but one cigar a day. But desire persecuted me every day and all day long. I found myself hunting for larger cigars ... within the month my cigar had grown to such proportions I could have used it as a crutch.' On another occasion, he described his habit during the five hours a day during which he wrote: 'I smoke with all my might, and allow no intervals.'

VAN DONGEN, KEES

The Dutch painter, who died in 1968, once wrote: 'The cigar, like the pipe, ought to match your physique.'

WAGNER, RICHARD

'You have unquestionably helped in my opera *Die Götterdämmerung*. This morning these marvels from Havana arrived and they immediately transported me to such enchantment as Pythia must have felt when she was enveloped in the vapours of Apollo.' So wrote the German composer on being given a gift of cigars.

WARNER, JACK

The great Hollywood studio boss, who with his three brothers founded Warner Brothers in 1923, was a famed smoker, in true film producer style. He preferred mild, pale cigars. He once won 100 million francs in the casino at Cannes, smoking a Hoyo de Monterrey panatela while he did it. He preserved the cigar in a silver box.

His cigar cutter, previously owned by Lord Mountbatten, was eventually acquired by director Francis Ford Coppola.

WAUGH, EVELYN

The novelist was an enthusiastic cigar smoker and bon vivant. The Partagas brand figures in *Brideshead Revisited*, and his diary has many references to cigar smoking – whether at home in Somerset, at White's Club in St James's or in restaurants such as Wiltons. He was often pictured smoking a cigar, and smoked while he worked. 'The most futile and disastrous day seems well spent when it is reviewed through the blue, fragrant smoke of a Havana.'

WAYNE, JOHN

'The Duke' was a famous cigar smoker in Hollywood, though he was relatively seldom seen smoking in his films.

WELLES, ORSON

Smoked cigars from the time his stupendous career took off with *Citizen Kane* in 1941 (when he was 26) until he died in 1985. He also smoked cigars in a number of movies such as *Touch of Evil*. Zino Davidoff recorded that he always demanded a box be opened before he bought it. "When refused, he grumbles but buys the whole box anyway. He has never complained about his purchases," Davidoff recalled. His favourite brand was Por Larranaga. Suitably, for a man of his eventual girth, he liked big cigars.

WOGAN, TERRY

The Irish-born talk show host was long one of the highest earners (if not the highest) on British television, and likes the good life – including a regular supply of Havana cigars.

Por Larranaga
Corona

WOOLF, VIRGINIA

The British novelist and critic, author of *Orlando* and *To The Lighthouse*, and founder member of the Bloomsbury Group (other members included economist Maynard Keynes, writers E.M. Forster and Lytton Strachey, and the painter Duncan Grant). The Bloosmbury Group believed in free living, and in this Virginia Woolf included smoking cigars.

ZANUCK, DARRYL F.

There are few pictures in existence of Darryl Zanuck without a cigar in either his hand or, more usually, his mouth. The legendary and restless film producer, who made *The Sun Also Rises*, *The Man in the Gray Flannel Suit* and *The Longest Day*, was a cigar connoisseur who even had an investment (along with Douglas Fairbanks and British film producer Sir Alexander Korda) in a Vuelta Abajo plantation, pre-Castro.

He liked dark, full-bodied *colorado* wrappers, on cigars such as the El Rey del Mundo Corona. He first started smoking cigars regularly in 1925 when, at the age of 23, he became head of production at Warner Brothers with a salary of $250,000 a year. He thought that smoking cigars (along with growing a moustache) would make him look older and give him a greater air of authority. Both the moustache and the cigars stayed with him for the rest of his life. He considered the best cigar of the day to be the first one he lit in the early evening. He would then chain-smoke them into the early hours while viewing rushes and poring over scripts. "I would rather die with a cigar in my mouth than boots on my feet," he told his doctor after suffering a stroke.

El Rey del Mundo
Corona

CIGAR
SUPPLIERS

LEADING CIGAR SHOPS

AUSTRALIA

ALEXANDER'S CIGAR DIVAN
at Crown Towers
8 Whiteman Street
Southbank
Melbourne
tel: 9292 7842

ALEXANDER'S CIGAR DIVAN
at Pierpoint's
Hotel Intercontinental
117 Macquarie Street
Sydney
tel: 9252 0280

ALFRED DUNHILL
74 Castlereagh Street
Sydney
tel: 9235 1600

BENJAMIN'S FINE TOBACCO
Shop 10 Strand Central
250 Elizabeth Street
Melbourne
tel: 9663 2879

SOL LEVY
713 George Street
Sydney
tel: 9211 5628

TUNNEY'S
38-40 Grote Street
Adelaide
tel: 8231 5720

AUSTRIA

CHRISTIAN KOZLIK
C.A.C. St Veit-Gasse 22
Vienna 1130
tel: 876 6449

CANADA

DAVIDOFF
1452 rue Sherbrooke W.
Montreal H3G 1K4
tel: 514 289 9118

GROUCHO & COMPANY
150 Bloor Street W.
Toronto M5S 2X9
tel: 416 922 4817

HAVANA HOUSE
87 Avenue Road
Toronto M5R 3R9
tel: 416 927 9070

MACDONALD TOBACCO &
GIFTS
1903 Barrington Street
Barrington Place
Halifax B3J 3L7
tel: 902 429 6872

THOMAS HINDS
TOBACCONIST
8 Cumberland Street
tel: 416 927 7703

TOBACCO HAVEN
595 Bay Street
Toronto M5C 2C2
tel: 416 593 6655

VANCOUVER CIGAR
COMPANY
1938 W. Broadway
Vancouver VJ6 1Z2
tel: 604 737 1313

DENMARK

W.O. LARSEN A/S
9 Amagertorv
Copenhagen DK-1160
tel: 312 2050

FINLAND

HAVANN-AITTA
Alexsanterinkatu 44
Helsinki
tel: 625 583

FRANCE

BOUTIQUE 22
22 avenue Victor-Hugo
Paris
tel: 45 01 81 41

LA CIVETTE
157 rue Saint-Honoré
Paris
tel: 42 96 04 99

LA RÉGENCE
10 cour du 30 Juillet
Bordeaux
tel: 56 81 63 44

LA TABAGIE
10 rue du Départ
Paris
tel: 45 38 65 18

LE KHÉDIVE
71 rue de la République
Lyons
tel: 78 37 86 95

LES QUATRE-TEMPS
Centre Commercial des
Quatre-Temps
La Défense
Paris
tel: 47 74 75 28

GERMANY

BERLIN

DAS TABAKHAUS
Im Forum Kopenick
Bahnhofstrasse 33-38
tel: 65 26 58 60

DAVIDOFF SHOP IM
KADEWE
Kaufhaus des Westens
Tauentzienstrasse 21-24
tel: 21 21 23 05

HAVANNA LOUNGE
CIGAR SHOP
Charlottenstrasse 35/36
tel: 206 10 80

KIWUS...NUR FÜR RAUCHER
Kantstrasse 56
tel: 312 44 50

PALM TOBACCO
Kurfürstendamm 214
tel: 881 57 94

PALM TOBACCO
Hohenzollerndamm 94
tel: 826 50 30

WOLFF TABAC &
CIGARS
Potsdamer Platz Arkaden
Alte Potsdamer Strasse 7
tel: 515 92 20

HAMBURG

M. NIEMEYER CIGARREN
Gerhofstrasse/Gänsemarkt
tel: 34 46 12

PFEIFEN TESCH
Colonnaden 10
tel: 34 25 84

TABACALERA HANSEATICA
Hanse-Viertel
Gr. Bleichen/Poststrasse 29
tel: 35 27 47

TOBACCO WORLD
Grosse Bleichen 1
tel: 35 18 49

WOLSDORFF TOBACCO
Spitalerstrasse 16
tel: 32 79 86

MUNICH

MAX ZECHBAUER
Residenzstrasse 10
tel: 29 68 86

STUTTGART

ALTE TABAKSTUBE RALPH
KNYRIM
Am Schillerplatz 4
tel: 29 27 29

DURNINGER-CLASSIC
Karlspassage/Breuninger
tel: 23 38 81

PFEIFEN-ARCHIV/DURNINGER
GMBH
Calwerpassage
tel: 29 07 01

HONG KONG

THE COHIBA CIGAR
DIVAN
The Mandarin Oriental Hotel
tel: 2522 0111

DAVIDOFF SHOP
Peninsula Hotel
Shop EL3
Salisbury Road
Kowloon
tel: 2368 5774

DAVIDOFF SHOP
Regent Hotel
Shop R106
Salisbury Road
Kowloon
tel: 2721 5520

SOGO DEPARTMENT STORE
555 Hennessey Road
Causeway Bay
tel: 2833 8338

IRELAND

J.J. FOX
119 Grafton Street
Dublin 2
tel: 459 363

ITALY

ACHILLE SAVINELLI SRL
Via Dogana 3
Milan 20123
tel: 875 100

SINCATO
34 Via de la Colonna
Antonina, Rome
tel: 785 55 08

NETHERLANDS

DAVIDOFF SHOP
Van Baerlestraat 84
1071 BB Amsterdam
tel: 671 1040

HAJENIUS
92-96 Rokin
Amsterdam
tel: 23 74 94

NORWAY

SOL CIGAR CO
Drammensun 8
255 Oslo
tel: 22 44 13 47

SPAIN

GIMENO
101 Paseo de Gracia
Barcelona
tel: 302 09 83

GONSALES DE LINARES
Paseo Habana no 26
Madrid
tel: 262 22 82

SANTIAGO
Calle Alcala no 18
Madrid
tel: 221 47 16

SWEDEN

BROBERGS TOBAKSHANDEL
AB
Sturegallerian 39
114 46 Stockholm
tel: 611 69 00

SWITZERLAND

BERNE

CIGARREN FLURY AG
Bahnhofplatz 3
tel: 311 37 03

CIGARREN FRIEDRICH & CO.
AG
Theaterplatz 2
tel: 311 72 81

GENEVA

ALFRED DUNHILL
rue de Rhône 59
tel: 312 42 60
DAVIDOFF & CIE
2 rue de Rive
tel: 310 90 41

GÉRARD PÈRE ET FILS
Hotel Noga Hilton
19 Quai du Mont-Blanc
tel: 732 65 11

TABAC RHEIN
rue du Mont-Blanc 1
tel: 732 4788

ZURICH

A DÜRR & CO. AG
Paradeplatz 3
tel: 211 07 36

CIGARES
Edisonstrasse 5
tel: 311 96 30

NAEGELI Z. TABAKFASS AG
Bellevue
Theaterstrasse 14
tel: 252 52 66

SCHWARZENBACH P. & CO.
Im Hauptbahnhof
tel: 211 63 25

TABAC SCHWARZENBACH
Löwenstrasse 68
tel: 211 40 40

UNITED KINGDOM

LONDON

ALFRED DUNHILL OF LONDON
48 Jermyn Street
SW1Y 6DL
tel: 020 7290 8606

ALFRED DUNHILL OF
LONDON
5 Royal Exchange
Cornhill
EC3V 3LL
tel: 020 7623 9977

BENSON & HEDGES
13 Old Bond Street
W1X 4QP
tel: 020 7493 1825

BURLINGTON BERTIE
57 Houndsditch
EC3A 8AA
tel: 020 7929 2242
website: www.bbertie-
cigars.com

DAVIDOFF OF LONDON
35 St. James's Street
SW1A 1HD
tel: 020 7930 3079

HARRODS CIGAR ROOM
Knightsbridge SW1X 7XL
tel: 020 7730 1234

HAVANA CLUB
165 Sloane Street
SW1X 9QB
tel: 020 7245 0890

JAMES J. FOX & ROBERT
LEWIS
19 St. James's Street
SW1A 1ES
tel: 020 7930 3787
website: www.jjfox.co.uk

SAUTTER OF MAYFAIR
106 Mount Street
Mayfair W1Y 5HE
tel: 020 7499 4866

THE SEGAR & SNUFF
PARLOUR
27a The Market
Covent Garden
WC2E 8RD
tel: 020 7836 8345

SELFRIDGES CIGAR
DEPARTMENT
400 Oxford Street
W1A 1AB
tel: 020 7629 1234

SHERVINGTONS
337 High Holborn
WC1V 7PX
tel: 020 7405 2929

TOMTOM
63 Elizabeth Street
Belgravia
SW1W 9PP
tel: 0207 730 1790
website: www.tomtom.co.uk

WALTER THURGOOD
161-162 Salisbury House
London Wall
EC2M 5QD
tel: 020 7628 5437

WARDS OF GRESHAM STREET
60 Gresham Street
EC2V 7BB
tel: 020 7606 4318
website: www.havana.co.uk

OUTSIDE LONDON

C. ASTON
Royal Exchange Shopping
Centre
Exchange Street
Manchester M2 7DB
tel: 0161 832 7895

CIGAR BOX
361 High Street
The Royal Mile
Edinburgh EH1 1PW
tel: 0131 225 3534

FREDERICK TRANTER
5 Church Street
Abbey Green
Bath BA1 1NL
tel: 01225 466197
website: www.tranter.co.uk

GAUNTLEYS OF NOTTINGHAM
4 High Street
Nottingham
NG1 2ET
tel: 0115 911 0555

GREENS OF LEEDS
37 The Headrow
Leeds
LS1 6PU
tel: 0113 244 4895

HARRISON & SIMMONDS OF
BEDFORD
80 High Street
Bedford
MK40 1NN
tel: 01234 266711
website: www.h-s.co.uk

HERBERT LOVE
31 Queensferry Street
Edinburgh
EH2 4QU
tel: 0131 225 8082

HERBERT LOVE
9 St. Vincent Place
Glasgow
G1 2DW
tel: 0141 226 4586

HOUSE OF MACKAY
6 Church Lane
Belfast
Northern Ireland
tel: 028 9024 6826

JOHN HOLLINGSWORTH
& SON
5 Temple Row
Birmingham
B2 5LG
tel: 0121 236 7768

LEWIS DARBEY & CO
12/14 Wyndham Arcade
Cardiff
CF10 1FJ
tel: 029 2023 3443

M. SHAVE
4/5 Harris Arcade
Reading
RG1 1DN
tel: 0118 959 5670

TAYLORS
19 Bond Street
Brighton
BN1 1RD
tel: 01273 606110

THE PIPE SHOP & LITTLE
HAVANA CIGAR STORE
92 & 76 Leith Walk
Edinburgh
EH6 5HB
tel: 0131 553 3561
website: www.thepipeshop.co.uk

TOBACCO WORLD
(Cheltenham)
Unit F7 Regent Arcade
Cheltenham
GL50 IJZ
tel: 01242 222037

UNITED STATES

BOSTON

ALFRED DUNHILL
69 Newbury Street
tel: 617 424 8600

CIGAR LANDING
Faneuil Hall Market
tel: 617 723 0147

HANOVER SMOKE SHOP
352 Hanover Street
tel: 617 523 2530

HOUSE OF CIGARS
262 Meridien Street
tel: 617 568 9737

THE HUMIDOR
800 Boylston Street
tel: 617 262 5510

CALIFORNIA

ALFRED DUNHILL
250 Post Road
San Francisco
tel: 415 781 3368

ALFRED DUNHILL
201 B North Rodeo Drive
Beverly Hills
tel: 310 274 5351

THE BEVERLY HILLS PIPE &
TOBACCO CO.
218 North Beverly Drive
Beverly Hills
tel: 310 276 3200

THE BIG EASY
12604 Ventura Boulevard
Studio City
tel: 818 762 3279

CALIFORNIA TOBACCO CENTER
1501 Polk Avenue
San Francisco
tel: 415 885 5479

CENTURY CITY TOBACCO
10250 Santa Monica
Boulevard
Los Angeles
tel: 310 277 0760

CHURCHILL'S FINE CIGARS
107 W. Broadway
Long Beach
tel: 310 491 7300

DAVIDOFF OF GENEVA
232 North Rodeo Drive
Beverly Hills
tel: 310 278 8884

GRANT'S
562 Market Street
San Francisco
tel: 415 981 1000

GUS'S SMOKE SHOP
13420 Ventura Boulevard
Sherman Oaks
tel: 818 789 1401

THE HUMIDOR
2201 Union Street
San Francisco
tel: 415 563 5181

NOB HILL CIGAR
699 Sutter Street
San Francisco
tel: 415 928 5799

CHICAGO

AROUND THE WORLD
TOBACCO
1044 West Belmont
tel: 773 327 7975

BLUE HAVANA
856 West Belmont
tel: 773 242 8262

CHICAGO CIGAR COMPANY
3843 N. Lincoln
tel: 773 929 2442

THE CIGAR SHOP AT NEIMAN-
MARCUS
737 N. Michigan Avenue
tel: 312 642 5900

GOODFELLAS CIGAR SHOP
5539 W. Montrose
tel: 773 286 9747

HABANA HOUSE OF FINE
CIGARS
5510 W. Devon
tel: 773 763 2130

IWAN RIES
19 S. Wabash
tel: 312 372 1306

JACK SCHWARTZ
175 W. Jackson
tel: 312 782 7898

RUBOVITS CIGARS
320 S. LaSalle
tel: 312 939 3780

MIAMI

CARIBBEAN CIGAR FACTORY
6265 SW. Eighth Street
tel: 305 267 3911

EL CREDITO
1106 SW Eighth Street
tel: 305 858 4162/800 726 9481

HAVANA HUMIDOR
7322 Red Road South
tel: 305 667 8749

NICK'S CIGAR COMPANY
7167 W. Flagler
tel: 305 266 9907

WORLD CIGARS
744 SW. Eighth Street
tel: 305 854 2110

NEW YORK

ALFRED DUNHILL
450 Park Avenue.
tel: 212 753 9292

ANGELO AND MAXIES
233 Park Avenue South
tel: 212 220 9207

ARNOLD'S
323 Madison Avenue
tel: 800 541 4545

BARCLAY REX
60 E. 42nd Street
tel: 212 692 9680

BARCLAY REX
570 Lexington Avenue
tel: 212 888 1015

DAVIDOFF OF GENEVA
535 Madison Avenue
tel: 212 751 9060

EASTSIDE CIGARS
969 Third Avenue
tel: 212 755 3255

FAMOUS SMOKE SHOP
55 W. 39th Street
tel: 212 221 1408/800 672 5544

H.R. SCOTT
64 Exchange Place
tel: 212 422 3046

HOME OF TOBACCO PRODUCTS
133 Eighth Avenue
tel: 212 989 3900

J. R. TOBACCO
11 E 45th Street
tel: 212 983 4160

J. R. TOBACCO
219 Broadway
tel: 212 233 6620

MOM'S CIGARS
172 Fifth Avenue
tel: 212 243 1943

NAT SHERMAN
500 Fifth Avenue
tel: 800 221 1690

TINDER BOX
500 Lexington Avenue
tel: 212 888 5071

PHILADELPHIA

BLACK CAT CIGAR COMPANY
1518 Sansom Street
tel: 215 563 9850

CITY CIGAR
2417 S. 11th Street
tel: 215 551 3662

HOLT'S CIGAR
12270 Townsend Avenue
tel: 800 523 1641

PHILADELPHIA CIGAR CO.
2506 Welsh Road
tel: 215 464 2222

TEXAS

ALFRED DUNHILL
The Galleria
5085 Westheimer Road
Houston
tel: 713 961 4661

CIGARZ CONNECTION
3611 A Greenville Avenue
Dallas
tel: 214 887 8840

CIGARS, PIPES & MORE
14520 Memorial Drive
Houston
tel: 713 493 9196

LONE STAR CIGARS
13305 Montfort Drive
Dallas
tel: 888 572 2427

RICHMOND AVENUE CIGARS
3301 Fondren Road
Houston
tel: 713 975 9057

STOGIES
6100 Westheimer Suite 102
Houston
tel: 713 780 9993

TOWN AND COUNTRY CIGARS
8204 Northeast Parkway 100
Fort Worth
tel: 817 427 1777

WASHINGTON D.C.

GEORGETOWN TOBACCO
3144 M Street NW.
tel: 202 338 5100

GRAND HAVANA ROOM
1220 19th Street NW.
tel: 202 293 6848

J.R. TOBACCO
1667 K Street NW.
tel: 202 296 3872

SIGNATURE CIGARS INC.
1817 M Street
tel: 202 822 1380

W. CURTIS DRAPER TOBACCO
640 14th Street NW.
tel: 202 638 2555

Cigar countries in Central America and the Caribbean

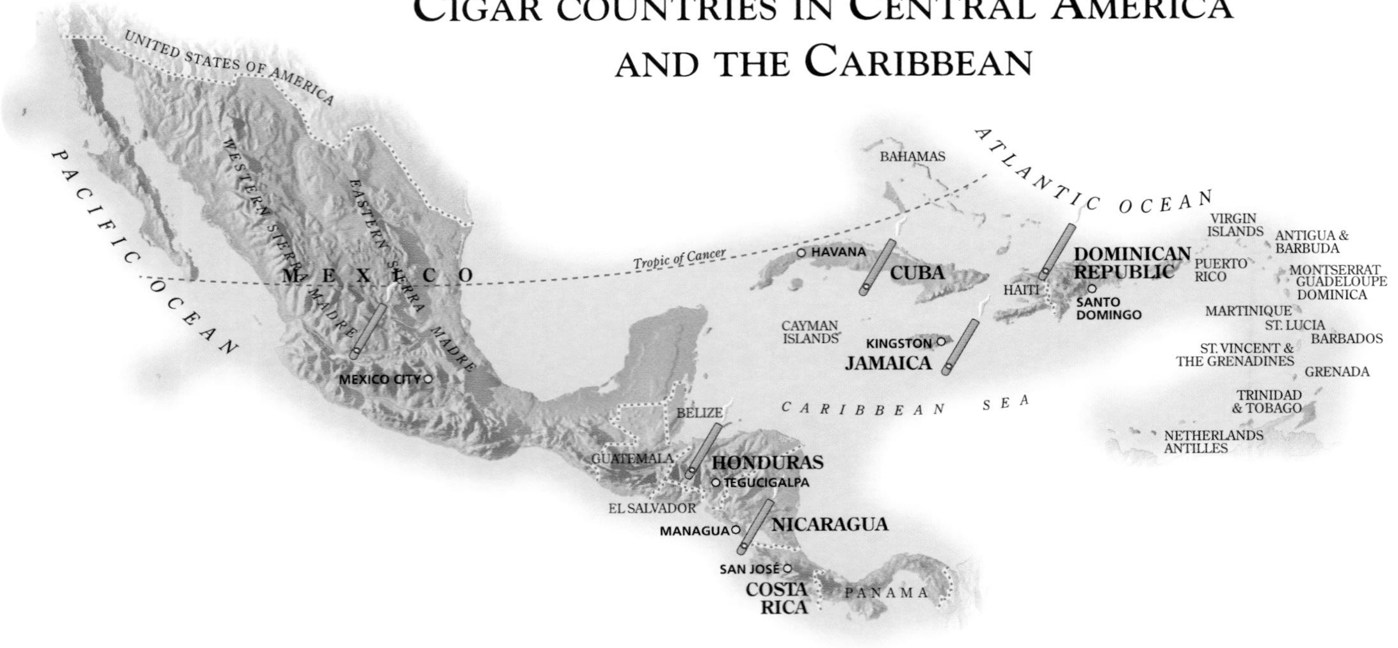

Cigar countries of the World

PHOTO CREDITS

AGIO SIGARENFABRIEKEN N.V.
BETTMANN/CORBIS
CHRISTINE OSBORNE: MEP
CHRISTIE'S IMAGES LTD 1999
CHURCHILL INTER-CONTINENTAL LONDON
CORBIS
DAVE ARMSTRONG
DAVIDOFF INTERNATIONAL
DAVIDOFF OF LONDON
DOMINICAN REPUBLIC TOURIST BOARD
FMG COMMUNICATIONS
HARRODS LTD
HARRY SMITH COLLECTION
HISTORICAL PICTURE ARCHIVE/CORBIS
HULTON-DEUTSCH COLLECTION/CORBIS
HUNTERS AND FRANKAU
IMAGE SELECT INTERNATIONAL LIMITED
JON WYAND
KURT KRIEGER/CORBIS
MONTE'S AND HAVANA CLUB
QUINTET PUBLISHING LTD
ROGER RESSMEYER/CORBIS
SCANTOURS LTD
SPANISH NATIONAL TOURIST OFFICE

SPECIAL THANKS

EDWARD SAHAKIAN
JAMES LEAVEY
JEAN CLARKE
MARIA STEWART
MARIE STEWART